Effective Ways
To Recruit And Retain
Minority Students

BY
Charles A. Taylor

Published by Praxis Publications, Inc.
P.O. Box 9869
Madison, Wisconsin 53715

Library of Congress Cataloging-in-Publication Data

Taylor, Charles A. (Charles Andrew)
    Effective ways to recruit and retain minority students
by Charles A. Taylor. -- New updated.

        Includes bibliographical references.
        ISBN 0-935483-05-5
        1. Minority college students--United States--Recruiting.
2. College attendance-- United States 3. College dropouts--
United States. I. Title. II. Title: New updated effective ways to
recruit and retain minority students.
LC3731.T37 1989
378'. 1982--dc20   89-36317
                                                    CIP

Praxis Publications, Inc., is an independent Multi-Cultural
Business Enterprise which publishes educational and cultural
literature; provides training programs, consultation and technical assistance to university and community groups. Praxis,
headquartered in Madison, Wisconsin, is emerging as a leader
in providing effective programs and services which seek to
improve the quality of education for all people. We invite you
to call or write us for additional information about our services
and products.

Third printing, 1989.

Acknowledgements:

Praxis gratefully acknowledges the following for their contributions to the completion of this book:

Individuals: Elizabeth Johanna, Charlie Taylor II, Wallace Evans Jr.

Departments: Department of Rural Sociology, UW-Madison, National Center for Educational Statistics, U.S. Census Bureau.

Cover and Book Design: Elizabeth Johanna

About the Author

Charles Taylor is currently the publisher and president of Praxis Publications, Inc., a publishing firm that publishes books and a wide range of literature pertaining to Minority Student services. Dr. Taylor earned his Ph. D at the University of Wisconsin-Madison, in Curriculum & Instruction-Educational Technology. He earned his Masters in Education from the University of Oregon and his B.S. from Southeast Missouri State University. He's been involved in student services for over a decade.

Charles has served as an Acting Assistant Vice Chancellor for Academic Support Services, director of a TRIO program, a director of a Multicultural Education Center, as an academic advisor, financial aid officer and a dorm counselor during his illustrious career. He has served as an advisor to many student organizations and is founder of Wisconsin's Annual Minority high School Student Leadership Conference. He continues to serve as a consultant to college campuses throughout America in the area of Minority Student Services.

TABLE OF CONTENTS

Introduction

This version of *Effective Ways to Recruit and Retain Minority Students* represents an expansion from our previous version.

We have included more detailed information about the Taylor Retention Model and included a self-evaluation instrument that allows campuses to assess seventeen critical program components ranging from Pre-Collegiate, the Freshmen Year, Financial Aids, to Affirmative Action Activities.

We've had a chance to observe dozens of programs firsthand and evaluate others. The results of these undertakings influenced our rewrite. We believe the new information provided offers the kind of guidance and assistance that will help campuses meet their equal educational opportunity goals.

This new version presents new ways to look at old problems. It allows campuses to become familiar with strategies that work.

This book reaffirms the adage that equity and quality are compatible; that is a university's standards are not lowered but actually strengthened by a strong retention program. A strong retention program usually results in more resources for faculty, efforts become targeted and people start to realize that it's a campus wide problem and not limited to certain offices.

Strong, effective retention programs should be encouraged and shared. Equal opportunity must not be allowed to become an abstraction. It will take commited people to make sure that never happens. Hopefully this book will help in that process.

Charles Taylor, Author

TAYLOR RETENTION MODEL

The recruitment and retention strategies presented in this book are based on a comprehensive model. For lack of a better name the retention model discussed is called the Taylor Retention Model (TRM).

The Taylor Retention Model is based on a holistic approach to recruiting and retaining minority students. The model is intended to serve as a guide for campuses presently engaged in ways to improve their retention rates. It covers in a substantive manner the various components (from pre-collegiate to alumni considerations) that must be addressed if recruitment and retention rates are to improve.

It is important to stress the relational nature of each area in the TRM and to urge readers to avoid the tendency of reducing an analyzation of the problem to simple parts in search of the ideal solution. Every link in the model is important. Each should be carefully studied in terms of current institutional practices. If your campus is lacking in a particular area, examples of successful ways to improve services are provided.

It's important to spell out clear objectives and expectation in each area of the model to help facilitate a smooth adjustment as the minority student moves through his/her collegiate experience.

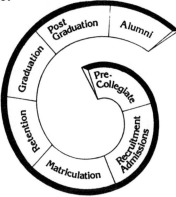

If your institution applies the model as recommended we sincerely believe you will experience effective ways to recruit and retain minority students.

WHY THE MODEL WORKS

A. The TRM uses a comprehensive approach in articulating the factors that impact retention and offers tested strategies to address these factors.

B. The TRM involves the entire campus thus preventing minority retention efforts from becoming ghettoized.

C. The model recognizes the vital role that faculty must play if retention efforts are to be meaningful.

D. The model is cyclical, highlighting the interdependence of each component.

E. The model emphasizes practical problem solving and improvement of current institutional practices. It includes those practices that have worked at other institutions while ommitting those that didn't.

F. The model is easy to follow and reproduce. Campus administrators find it "user friendly" in assessing what they're currently doing and its guidelines help them to establish effective priorities.

G. The model recognizes significant social problems and offers remedies to reduce barriers.

H. The model is grounded in research, tested on many college campuses and updated regularly as new ground is cleared in the field.

I. The model permits self-evaluation and allows administrators to determine what is proper and adequate for their institution.

PRE-COLLEGIATE ISSUES
_____

Recent studies have indicated that it's never too
early to begin preparing youngsters for college. A 1984
study published by the High-Scope Educational Research
Foundation of Ypsilanti, Michigan, found that pre-school
programs help kids through life. The study found that youngsters who attended pre-school had higher employment, high
school and college graduation rates, performed better on
tests, were in less trouble with the law and in general contributed more to society. It should be kept in mind that college
has not been a "family experience" for most minority students. Therefore it often takes targeted efforts to get them
thinking about college at an early age.

A pre-college program can be to campuses what Head
Start programs are to elementary schools. Both programs are
designed to prepare students for a successful schooling
experience. They assess student's academic weaknesses and
strengths and provide assistance to overcome deficiences.

Data suggests that these programs work, and they work
well. The Wadleigh Junior High School in central Harlem is a
good example. Recently celebrating its twentieth year it has
prepared students from the neighborhood to get into prestig-
ious preparatory schools and then on to the top universities in
the country.

Administrators and teachers work with seven and
eighth graders after school to tone up their math and reading
skills. Students are also exposed to a wide range of cultural and social activities. The program has been very effective in motivating youngsters, in building character and in
enhancing ambition. The Wadleigh program is associated
with the national nonprofit *A Better Chance* program which
also indentifies and places talented minority youngsters into
private schools.

Another pre-collegiate program worth mentioning
is the Principal's Scholars Program (PSP) that began in
Chicago by administrators at the University of Illinois at

Champaign-Urbana and today extends throughout the state. This program was created to increase the pool of minority high school graduates able to pursue higher education. Principals identify most PSP participants in eighth grade. With their parents approval, the students commit themselves to the stringent academic requirements of the program in high school. Competition is keen among the schools who want the best students and recruit to get them. Students participate in monthly enrichment programs given by minority speakers. They participate in math, science, essay and speech contests and take field trips to universities, industries and theaters. At the end of the year recognition banquets are held at some of the schools.

Perhaps the most successful pre-collegiate programs are Upward Bound type programs in which middle and high school students actually live on campus, take college courses, and interact with faculty. According to a report written by Deltha Colvin (Assistant Dean of Students/Special Programs at Wichita State University),

> Upward Bound programs have been extremely effective in motivating "disadvantaged" high school students to attend and graduate from college. Four years after high school graduation, Upward Bound participants are four times more likely to earn a baccalaureate degree as compared to non-participants, (Colvin,1984).

A characteristic that successful pre-college programs have in common is clear objectives. Several years ago Central Florida Community College's Special Services program listed the following specific program objectives.

Academic:
- to increase reading ability to a (measurable pre and post-test) minimum acceptable level.
- to improve writing ability to a minimum acceptable level.
- to improve the ability to identify and solve social problems.

- to develop math skills necessary for academic and career success.
- to develop successful study skills.

Student support:
- to assist the student in dealing with the red tape of college procedures and regulations.
- to provide assistance in obtaining financial support.
- to assist in finding solutions to personal problems hindering academic success.
- to assist the student in obtaining needed medical information and aid.
- to enlist the aid of the community in fulfilling student needs.

Affective domain:
- to improve the self-concept and attitude toward self.
- to integrate the student into the mainstream of the cultural and academic college process.
- to foster faculty, staff and community acceptance and respect for the student.
- to develop an awareness of educational or career goals.

Whether they are able to accomplish all of the above is open to debate. Nonetheless, this is a comprehensive approach to addressing the needs of pre-collegiate students.

The issue of pre-collegiate programs takes on a special significance in light of increased minority elementary/middle school enrollment projections. For the forseeable future the number of minority school age children is expected to increase. The society can ill afford the waste of so many young minds and talents.

The consequences of such a benign neglect policy means greater minority unemployment, higher incidences of poverty and the possibility of being relegated to a permanent underclass.

A strong argument has been waged that if the public schools carried out their responsibility, pre-collegiate programs would not be necessary. Although that argument appears to be persuasive, it's fairly safe to say a great deal of time will probably pass before public schools "advantage" minority students.

In recent years there have been greater calls for accountability as some communities contemplate linking more closely administrators and teacher's jobs with children's achievement.

High Dropout Rate

The factor that can't be ignored (if enrollment rates are to increase) is the high dropout/pushout rate among Minority youngsters beginning in middle school. The high dropout rate is a national crisis in education which requires immediate and long term attention. The best recruiting plans can end up in shambles if the applicant pool is depleted by high dropout rates.

City schools have dropout rates far exceeding national averages. More than half the students fail to finish in some schools and overall dropout rates of 40 percent are commonly reported, (Catterall, 1986).

Table 1 provides information on national dropout rates. Although there was some improvement during the decade dropout is still at extremely high levels in urban areas. The critical years seem to be during the ages of 16 and 17 for all students.

The costs of addressing the dropout problem suggests that a dollar of public investment, if effectively spent, might have brought society nearly five dollars in national income, (Catterall, 1986 p. 11).

Table 1

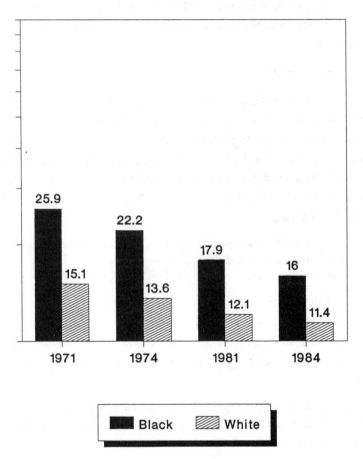

PERCENT OF HIGH SCHOOL DROPOUTS BY RACE
Among Persons 14-34 years old

Dropouts are persons not enrolled in
school and who aren't high school grads

Sources: Adapted from U.S. Dept. of Commerce, Bureau of
Census, Current Population Reports, Series P-20, No. 241 and
No. 373.

Table 2

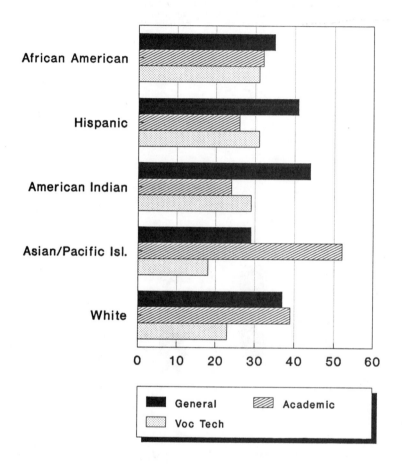

HIGH SCHOOL PROGRAM ENROLLMENT BY RACE

Because of rounding totals may not add
up to 100%

Source: adapted from U.S. Dept. of Education, National Center for Education
Statistics, survey of High School and Beyond, 1980. (Table 61)

It seems that substantial proportions of Blacks, Hispanics and Indians
are in nonacademic high school programs which could pose a serious problem
in increasing the minority college student ranks.

The curriculum that is offered a substantial proportion of Blacks, Hispanics and Indians is in weak-academic areas.

Table 2 shows that only Asian Americans enroll in academic areas more than they do in general or vocational classes. This poses a serious problem in increasing the minority college student ranks. Watered down curriculums won't give students the skills they need to meet stringent academic standards. What may be even more distressing is what appeared in Lorenzo Morris's study (1979). He found that Black high school students appear to be "less aware" than other high school students of the pre-requisite courses for admission to higher education. Morris also found that a significant proportion of Black high school students think that they are enrolled in college preparatory courses when they are not. Clearly intervention strategies are needed if this misconception is to be changed. Add to that the growing number of states requiring competency tests and Universities raising admission requirements and the results are predictable.

If your campus does not have a pre-college program we would strongly recommend that you establish one. These programs have an impressive track record. They have demonstrated convincingly that students who participate in them stand a better chance of graduating than students who don't.

Pre-College Initiatives

In addition to upward bound programs some campuses have initiated the following types of activities.
- Allowed academically talented minority youngsters to register as guest students while still in high school with the under standing that courses taken would count for degree credit upon their admission.
- Initiated informational programs in minority communities, schools etc,.

- Provided computer, science and/or engineering camps for minority youngsters.
- Established a toll-free line to provide information about their campus.
- Produced dial-a-tapes that answer a variety of questions (from the minority perspective) about their institution.
- Established liasons with elementary and secondary teaching associations.
- Sponsored joint pre-collegiate programs with other colleges. This works well in large cities where there may be several colleges in close proximity.
- Hosted "College for Kids" programs during the summer or designated weekends for youngsters.
- Developed feeder schools in an effort to create a tradition of students from the feeder school attending their University.
- Established contact directly with minority youngsters in middle school and maintained correspondence with them as they progressed through high school.

Innovative Pre-College Programs

The programs listed in this section were taken from press releases and campus newspapers. They are included to give you ideas about successful programs.

Harlem and Science

The Harlem Public Service Science Center at City College conducts Harlem Town Meetings on science education for students, parents and teachers from the local community. The meetings include workshops in computer science, life science, physical science and engineering as well as film demonstrations and question and answer sessions with experts.

Project Uplift

Project Uplift, an annual program designed to acquaint minority students with the University of North Carolina

(UNC) attracts over 700 high school seniors during weekend sessions. A letter is sent by UNC to every high school guidance counselor in the state. In return the guidance counselors send a list of student names with academic potential and their participation in extracurricular activities. UNC officials predict that over 60 percent of the students who participate in Project Uplift eventually attend UNC.

High School Students Honored

The University of Connecticut asks principals, teachers, and counselors from more than 250 schools throughout the state to nominate out-standing minority high schools students to be honored at the University of Connecticut's Day of Pride. The Day of Pride has proven to be an effective method to enhance minority students interest in attending U-Conn. Several criteria are considered before a student is nominated, including community involvement, work experience, demonstrated leadership and academic performance.

Pre-Engineering Program

Massachussetts Pre-Engineering Program for Minority Students Inc. (MASS PEP) is a private industry initative in the Boston and Cambridge area to assist minority students in acquiring academic preparation and disciplines needed for careers in engineering, the sciences and technology. MASS PEP requires its students to complete a full four-year sequence in mathematics, science and the language arts. In return MASS PEP offers an incentive program to recognize and award achievement. Student progress is closely monitored in the program.

Science Seminar For Minority Students

West Virginia holds an annual Health Science Seminar for Minority and other Middle School students of West Virginia. The seminar is available at no charge to the participants. The students stay on campus and are exposed to health career options, told about the necessary college preparatory courses, and meet with health professionals in their work environment.

Staying In School Forum

Black professionals from ten disciplines spoke to area black high school students at the University of Illinois Champaign- Urbana's 8th annual forum on Higher Education. Delta Sigma Theta sponsored the forum to encourage students "to stay in high school and go on to college to pursue professional careers".

Campus Workshops Offered

Community Workshops on the benefits of and opportunities for a college education are offered by San Francisco State University's office of Student Affirmative Action. The workshops entitled "Invest in Your Child's Future" are designed for students in grades 8 through 12 and the parents of students enrolled in the San Francisco Unified School District.

Student Visiting Days

Mills College in Oakland, California sponsors student visiting days for high school sophomores and junior females. Activities include a campus tour, admission and financial aid sessions, student panels, and round-table faculty discussions.

Apprenticeship Program Gives Minority Students Research Experience

Fourteen high school students participated in the summer research apprenticeship program sponsored by the Office of Minority Affairs at the University of Kansas. The young research assistants were paid $140 a week for the eight-week program. The program was made possible through grants given by the National Institute of Health and the National Science Foundation.

Pre-Collegiate Resources

There are a number of model pre-college programs for campuses to emulate. Contacting the National Council of Educational Opportunity Associations (NCEOA) at 1025 Vermont Avenue, NW, Suite 310, Washington, DC 20005, 202/ 347-7430 is a good starting point. They can recommend effective programs, provide information on member projects and provide guidance on obtaining funding for such programs.

A Better Chance
419 Boylston St.
Boston, MA 02116 617/536-5270
Helps recruit talented minority students for colleges and public school programs.

National Alliance of Black School Educators
2816 Georgia Ave., NW
Washington, DC 20001 202/483-1549
Organization of Black educators, majority of which are elementary and secondary officials.

National Chicano Council for Higher Education
710 N. College Ave.
Claremont, CA 91711 714/625-6607 or 624-9594

National Association for Bilingual Education
1201 16th St., Room 408, NW
Washington, DC 20036 202/822-7870

National Association for Equal Opportunity in Higher Education
Lovejoy Bldg., Suite 207
400 12th St., NE
Washington, DC 20002 202/543-9111

Trends in College Enrollment: 1972-1982

Each fall the National Center for Education Statistics (NCES) conducts a survey of enrollment in colleges, universities, and professional schools throughout the country. In October each year the Bureau of the Census, in its current population survey, obtains data on the demographic characteristics of college students. When the statistics for fall 1982 are compared with those a decade earlier, some interesting trends in college enrollment emerge.

According to the NCES surveys, college enrollment increased from 9.2 million in fall 1972 to 12.4 million in fall 1982. The Bureau of the Census figures are quite similar. Both agencies reported a total enrollment increase of about 35 percent over the past decade. As Table 3 indicates, however, there were major differences in the rate of increase in college attendance among the various groups represented in the surveys. Growth rates appear to be high for black and other racial minorities, persons 25 years old and over, students in 2-year institutions, part-time students, and women. They were lower for men, full-time students, persons 18 to 24 years old, students in universities and other 4-year institutions, and white students. The rate of growth was slightly above average for students in publicly controlled institutions and somewhat below average for those in private colleges and universities.

The proportion of college students who were women rose from 43.1 percent in 1972 to 51.5 percent in 1982. Black and other races represented 10.4 percent of the total enrollment in 1972 compared with 14.3 percent a decade later. Students 25 years of age and over accounted for 28.0 percent of enrollment in 1972 and for 35.6 percent of the total in 1982. Part-time students constituted 34.1 percent of the entire student body in 1972 compared with 41.9 percent in 1982.

Two-year colleges increased their share of total enrollment from 29.9 percent in 1972 to 38.4 percent in 1982.
Publicly controlled institutions enrolled 76.7 percent of the
students a decade earlier, compared with 78.0 percent in 1982.

More detailed information on college enrollment may
be found in the NCES reports on "Fall Enrollment in Colleges
and Universities" and in the Bureau of the Census reports on
"School Enrollment-Social and Economic Characteristics of
Students".

Also the July 23, 1986 issue of "the Chronicle of Higher
Education" (p. 25-34) provides a detailed account of the racial
make-up of college and university enrollment up to 1984.

RECRUITMENT/ADMISSIONS ISSUES

Table 3

   While Blacks and other minorities experienced great
gains during the decade, the figures may be misleading. Generally speaking the number of Blacks attending college the past
5 years has declined, the number receiving college degrees
has declined and the attrition rates have increased. Much of
this is evidenced on the following pages in this chapter.

PERCENTAGE INCREASE IN THE ENROLLMENT OF
COLLEGE STUDENTS WITH SELECTED CHARACT.

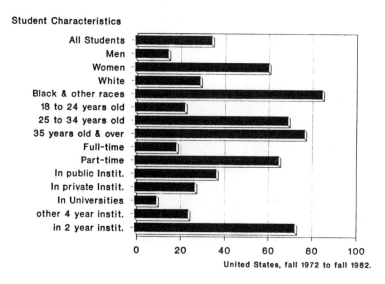

Student Characteristics

United States, fall 1972 to fall 1982.

Sources: U.S. Bureau for the Census, the National Center for
Education Statistics, US DOE. (1983)

Table 4

Table 4 shows the beginning of the decline of Black students that has continued throughout the 80's. Other groups have remained fairly consistent.

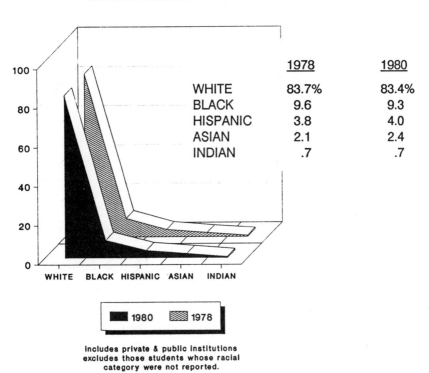

TOTAL ENROLLMENT IN INSTITUTIONS OF
HIGHER EDUCATION BY RACE

	1978	1980
WHITE	83.7%	83.4%
BLACK	9.6	9.3
HISPANIC	3.8	4.0
ASIAN	2.1	2.4
INDIAN	.7	.7

Includes private & public institutions
excludes those students whose racial
category were not reported.

Sources: adapted from U.S. Department of Education, National Center for Education Statistics, special tabulation from the surveys of *Fall Enrollment in Higher Education*, 1978 and 1980.

Table 5

Table 5 shows that 70% of the states fail to enroll the percentage of Minority students equivalent to the percentage of Minority population in their state. States in the Northeast do a better job than those in the other regions.

State	Percentage of Minority Population by State (1980)	Percentage of Minority College Enrolled by State (1984)
Alabama	26.8	22.8
Alaska	23.7	14.9
Arizona	25.4	17.0
Arkansas	17.8	16.8
California	33.0	29.6
Colorado	16.9	10.8
Connecticut	11.7	8.3
Delaware	18.6	12.6
Dist. of Columbia	74.1	39.3
Florida	23.3	21.3
Georgia	28.5	21.5
Hawaii	69.9	70.7
Idaho	5.9	4.7
Illinois	21.7	19.4
Indiana	9.6	8.2
Iowa	2.8	4.3
Kansas	9.3	8.7
Kentucky	8.2	8.8
Louisiana	32.6	26.7
Maine	1.3	1.4
Maryland	25.9	21.5
Massachusetts	7.3	8.0
Michigan	15.7	12.7
Minnesota	3.6	3.9
Mississippi	36.7	30.1
Missouri	12.2	10.5
Montana	6.5	6.3
Nebraska	5.8	5.1
Nevada	16.5	12.3
New Hampshire	1.5	2.7
New Jersey	20.7	18.2
New Mexico	47.1	33.5
New York	25.1	20.8
North Carolina	32.7	20.6
North Dakota	4.3	5.2
Ohio	11.6	10.1
Oklahoma	14.8	12.7
Oregon	6.2	7.3
Pennsylvania	10.7	9.4
Rhode Island	5.8	5.9
South Carolina	32.0	22.2
South Dakota	7.6	7.6
Tennessee	16.9	15.8
Texas	34.1	25.4
Utah	7.1	5.2
Vermont	1.3	2.1
Virginia	21.7	17.3
Washington	9.4	9.8
West Virginia	4.3	5.2
Wisconsin	6.2	6.3
Wyoming	7.8	4.0

Source: U.S. Census Bureau

Where do we find minority students?

Universities and colleges must answer three distinct but interrelated questions regarding minority students recruitment and admissions: "Where do we find minority students? How do we recruit them?" and, "What things do we consider before we admit them?" The way in which individual institutions respond to these questions determines whether their recruitment strategies are effective or not.

While the White student population between the ages of 16-24 is projected to decrease into the 1990's, the minority student population is expected to increase.

Tables at the end of this section provide information on location of potential students. For example Census data points out that the majority of Chicanos are located in the southwest and Blacks in the south and urban areas. The question then becomes (for states with low minority population), how do we deal with the non-resident tuition problem? In determining applicant pools, we would recommend that you figure out what percentage of your currently enrolled white students are non-resident and establish minority non-resident parity figures based on that percentage. The issue of financial aids will be addressed later.

Some universities have created targeted recruitment programs. These include a computerized applicant pool that lists the names of not only their state's minority students but prospective minority students across the nation. Others have developed fairly sophisticated marketing strategies which include tapping into the network established by predominantly Black institutions. Still others have found success by utilizing non-traditional sources such as Department of Social Service Workers, public housing employees, CETA/JPTA officials, county welfare departments and neighborhood hang outs.

Universities must begin to consider the older nontraditional student as well. Although their study did not concentrate soley on minority students, Henderson and Plummer found that *"only half of the college going population at the end of the 1970s entered directly from high school"* (Henderson & Plummer, 1978, p. 25).

The issue of minority student recruitment begs for creativity on the part of institutions of higher learning. As was alluded to earlier, there are several barriers that must be dealt with if campuses hope to establish realistic recruiting goals; financial aid and the atrocious drop out rate among Black, Hispanic and Indian students.

The data shows that in 1978 nearly a fourth of Black Americans between 16 and 34 were not in school and had not graduated from high school. The question of where do we find them becomes increasingly complex as a result of the drop out rates.

Tables 6-18 include Minority population figures by state. They answer the question, "where do we find them?".

Table 6

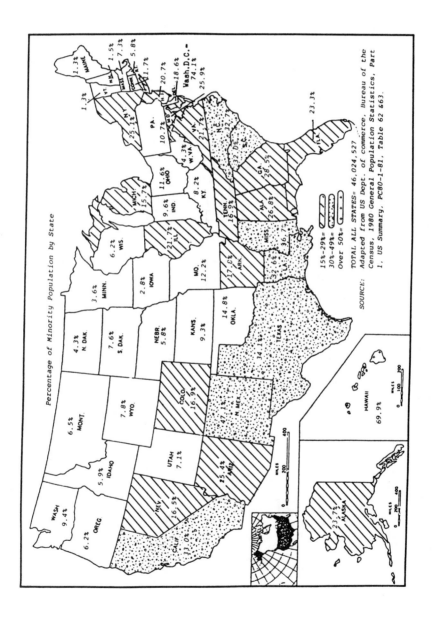

Table 7

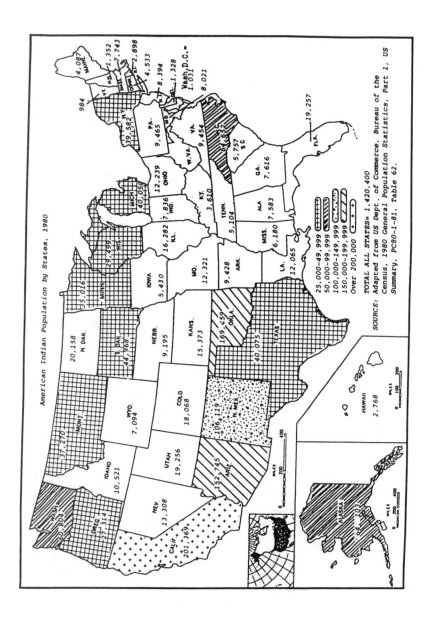

American Indian Population by States, 1980

SOURCE: Adapted from US Dept. of Commerce, Bureau of the Census, 1980 General Population Statistics, Part 1, US Summary, PC80-1-81, Table 62.

TOTAL ALL STATES= 1,420,400

Table 8

American Indian Population Ranked by Rural Portion of State-1980			Percent American Indian Ranked by Rural Portion of State-1980		
Rank	State	American Indian Population	Rank	State	Percent American Indian
1.	Arizona	104,502	1.	Arizona	23.8%
2.	Oklahoma	85,356	2.	New Mexico	20.6
3.	New Mexico	74,660	3.	South Dakota	9.0
4.	North Carolina	50,275	4.	Oklahoma	8.6
5.	California	36,963	5.	Alaska	8.3
6.	South Dakota	33,132	6.	Montana	7.4
7.	Montana	27,405	7.	North Dakota	4.8
8.	Washington	25,343	8.	Nevada	4.4
9.	North Dakota	16,000	9.	Utah	3.9
10.	Wisconsin	15,695	10.	Wyoming	2.9
11.	Minnesota	14,515	11.	Washington	2.3
12.	Michigan	14,344	12.	California	1.8
13.	New York	11,932	13.	North Carolina	1.6
14.	Alaska	11,898	14.	Idaho	1.6
15.	Oregon	11,152	15.	Oregon	1.3
16.	Utah	8,857	16.	Minnesota	1.1
17.	Texas	7,564	17.	Wisconsin	0.9
18.	Idaho	7,015	18.	Colorado	0.9
19.	Louisiana	5,970	19.	Nebraska	0.8
20.	Nevada	5,199	20.	Kansas	0.6
21.	Arkansas	4,993	21.	Michigan	0.5
22.	Wyoming	4,988	22.	Delaware	0.5
23.	Florida	4,947	23.	Louisiana	0.5
24.	Colorado	4,913	24.	Arkansas	0.5
25.	Mississippi	4,721	25.	New York	0.4
26.	Kansas	4,462	26.	Maine	0.4
27.	Nebraska	4,427	27.	Rhode Island	0.4
28.	Missouri	4,325	28.	Mississippi	0.4
29.	Alabama	4,220	29.	Florida	0.3
30.	South Carolina	3,345	30.	Hawaii	0.3
31.	Georgia	2,854	31.	Missouri	0.3
32.	Ohio	2,766	32.	Alabama	0.3
33.	Virginia	2,747	33.	Texas	0.3
34.	Maine	2,604	34.	South Carolina	0.2
35.	Pennsylvania	2,326	35.	Vermont	0.2
36.	Indiana	2,321	36.	New Jersey	0.2
37.	Illinois	2,148	37.	Massachusetts	0.2
38.	Tennessee	2,036	38.	Maryland	0.2
39.	Massachusetts	1,624	39.	Virginia	0.2
40.	Iowa	1,518	40.	New Hampshire	0.1
41.	New Jersey	1,443	41.	Georgia	0.1
42.	Kentucky	1,360	42.	Iowa	0.1
43.	Maryland	1,333	43.	Connecticut	0.1
44.	West Virginia	1,019	44.	Indiana	0.1
45.	Delaware	839	45.	Illinois	0.1
46.	Connecticut	796	46.	Tennessee	0.1
47.	Vermont	631	47.	Ohio	0.1
48.	New Hampshire	616	48.	West Virginia	0.1
49.	Rhode Island	498	49.	Kentucky	0.1
50.	Hawaii	389	50.	Pennsylvania	0.1
51.	Dist. of Col.	0	51.	Dist. of Col.	0.0
Total		644986	Total		1.1%

Source: U.S. Bureau of the Census, 1980 Census of Population, General Population Characteristcs, PC80-1-B1, Table 62.

Table 9

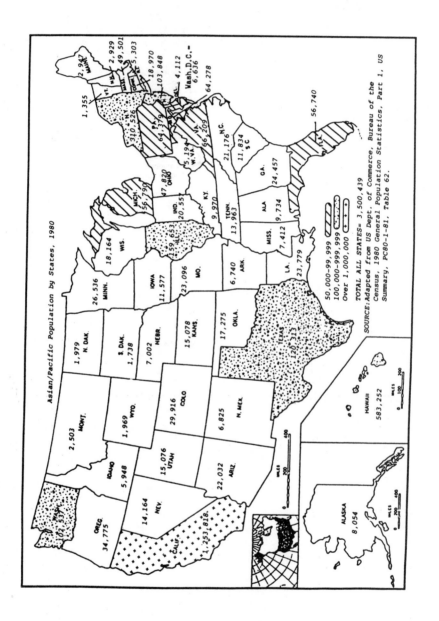

Asian/Pacific Population by States, 1980

TOTAL ALL STATES= 3,500,439

SOURCE: Adapted from US Dept. of Commerce, Bureau of the Census, 1980 General Population Statistics, Part 1, US Summary, PC80-1-81, Table 62.

50,000–99,999
100,000–999,999
Over 1,000,000

Table 10

Asian & Pacific Islander Population Ranked by Rural Portion of State - 1980		Percent Asian & Pacific Islander Ranked by Rural Portion of State - 1980	
Rank State	Asian & Pacific Islander Population	Rank State	Percent American Indian
1. Hawaii	75,273	1. Hawaii	57.9%
2. California	35,428	2. Alaska	23.7
3. Alaska	33,982	3. California	1.7
4. Washington	8,412	4. New Jersey	0.8
5. New York	7,927	5. Nevada	0.8
6. Pennsylvania	7,750	6. Washington	0.8
7. New Jersey	6,834	7. Oregon	0.6
8. Texas	6,706	8. Connecticut	0.4
9. Michigan	6,135	9. Utah	0.4
10. Ohio	4,925	10. Idaho	0.4
11. Oregon	4,689	11. Delaware	0.4
12. North Carolina	4,321	12. Maryland	0.4
13. Illinois	4,211	13. Colorado	0.4
14. Florida	4,083	14. Massachusetts	0.4
15. Massachusetts	3,621	15. Rhode Island	0.4
16. Virginia	3,463	16. Arizona	0.4
17. Indiana	3,448	17. New York	0.3
18. Maryland	3,442	18. Florida	0.3
19. Georgia	3,297	19. New Hampshire	0.2
20. Minnesota	3,069	20. Kansas	0.2
21. Connecticut	2,944	21. Texas	0.2
22. Missouri	2,528	22. Minnesota	0.2
23. Louisiana	2,518	23. Michigan	0.2
24. Wisconsin	2,356	24. Illinois	0.2
25. Colorado	2,190	25. Pennsylvania	0.2
26. West Virginia	1,982	26. Wyoming	0.2
27. South Carolina	1,948	27. Montana	0.2
28. Tennessee	1,905	28. Louisiana	0.2
29. Idaho	1,900	29. Virginia	0.2
30. Kansas	1,887	30. Vermont	0.2
31. Mississippi	1,779	31. Indiana	0.2
32. Kentucky	1,767	32. Nebraska	0.2
33. Iowa	1,766	33. Ohio	0.2
34. Arizona	1,563	34. Missouri	0.2
35. Oklahoma	1,460	35. Maine	0.2
36. Alabama	1,458	36. Georgia	0.2
37. Arkansas	1,316	37. West Virginia	0.2
38. New Hampshire	1,082	38. New Mexico	0.2
39. Nebraska	1,001	39. Oklahoma	0.1
40. Utah	1,001	40. Iowa	0.1
41. Maine	948	41. North Carolina	0.1
42. Nevada	930	42. Wisconsin	0.1
43. Montana	755	43. South Carolina	0.1
44. Delaware	744	44. Mississippi	0.1
45. Vermont	640	45. North Dakota	0.1
46. New Mexico	571	46. Arkansas	0.1
47. Rhode Island	471	47. South Dakota	0.1
48. North Dakota	441	48. Tennessee	0.1
49. South Dakota	410	49. Kentucky	0.1
50. Wyoming	371	50. Alabama	0.1
51. Dist. of Col.	0	51. Dist. of Col.	0.0
Total	273,648	Total	0.5%

Source: U.S. Bureau of the Census, 1980 Census of Population, General Population Characteristics, PC80-1-B1, Table 62.

Table 11

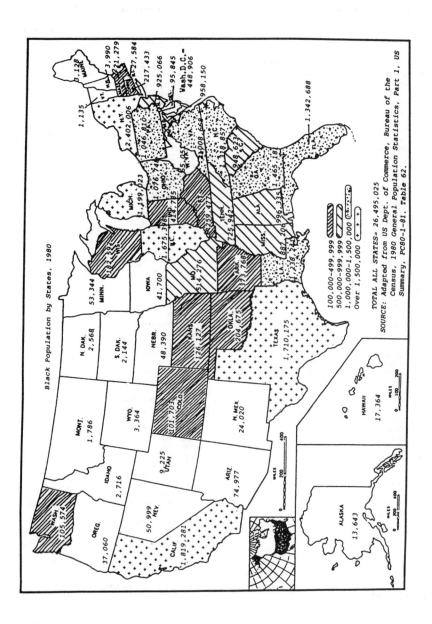

Black Population by States, 1980

TOTAL ALL STATES= 26,495,025

SOURCE: Adapted from US Dept. of Commerce, Bureau of the Census, 1980 General Population Statistics, Part 1, US Summary, PC80-1-81, Table 62.

100,000-499,999
500,000-999,999
1,000,000-1,500,000
Over 1,500,000

Table 12

Black Population Ranked by Rural Portion of State-1980		Percent Black Ranked by Rural Portion of State-1980	

Rank State	Black Population	Rank State	Percent Black
1. North Carolina	568,675	1. Mississippi	35.3%
2. Mississippi	468,347	2. South Carolina	32.5
3. South Carolina	465,477	3. Louisina	22.7
4. Georgia	389,212	4. Alabama	19.4
5. Virginia	308,493	5. Georgia	18.9
6. Alabama	301,802	6. North Carolina	18.6
7. Louisina	299,479	7. Virginia	17.0
8. Texas	202,194	8. Delaware	15.0
9. Florida	162,746	9. Maryland	12.3
10. Arkansas	127,914	10. Arkansas	11.6
11. Maryland	102,508	11. Florida	10.6
12. Tennessee	101,927	12. Texas	7.0
13. California	38,607	13. Tennessee	5.6
14. New Jersey	38,338	14. New Jersey	4.8
15. Kentucky	38,238	15. Oklahoma	2.3
16. New York	33,050	16. Kentucky	2.1
17. Michigan	32,172	17. West Virginia	2.1
18. Pennsylvania	27,778	18. California	1.9
19. Ohio	26,670	19. Missouri	1.3
20. West Virginia	26,287	20. New York	1.2
21. Delaware	26,110	21. Michigan	1.2
22. Oklahoma	22,704	22. Connecticut	1.1
23. Missouri	20,131	23. Arizona	1.0
24. Illinois	19,495	24. Illinois	1.0
25. Massachusetts	7,677	25. Ohio	0.9
26. Indiana	7,532	26. Alaska	0.9
27. Connecticut	7,021	27. Massachusetts	0.8
28. Kansas	5,334	28. Nevada	0.8
29. Arizona	4,602	29. Pennsylvania	0.8
30. Washington	3,779	30. Kansas	0.7
31. Wisconsin	2,556	31. Hawaii	0.6
32. New Mexico	1,445	32. New Mexico	0.4
33. Colorado	1,425	33. Indiana	0.4
34. Oregon	1,378	34. Washington	0.3
35. Alaska	1,301	35. Rhode Island	0.3
36. Iowa	1,012	36. Colorado	0.3
37. New Hampshire	981	37. New Hampshire	0.2
38. Minnesota	911	38. Oregon	0.2
39. Nevada	908	39. Vermont	0.2
40. Hawaii	832	40. Wisconsin	0.2
41. Maine	767	41. Maine	0.1
42. Nebraska	672	42. Utah	0.1
43. Vermont	525	43. Nebraska	0.1
44. South Dakota	384	44. Wyoming	0.1
45. Rhode Island	378	45. South Dakota	0.1
46. Idaho	369	46. Idaho	0.1
47. Utah	281	47. Iowa	0.1
48. Wyoming	189	48. Minnesota	0.1
49. Montana	188	49. Montana	0.1
50. North Dakota	158	50. North Dakota	0.0
51. Dist. of Col.	0	51. Dist. of Col.	0.0
Total	3,901,009	Total	6.6%

Source: U.S. Bureau of the Census, 1980 Census of Population, General Population Characteristics, PC80-1-B1, Tables 62 and 63.

Table 13

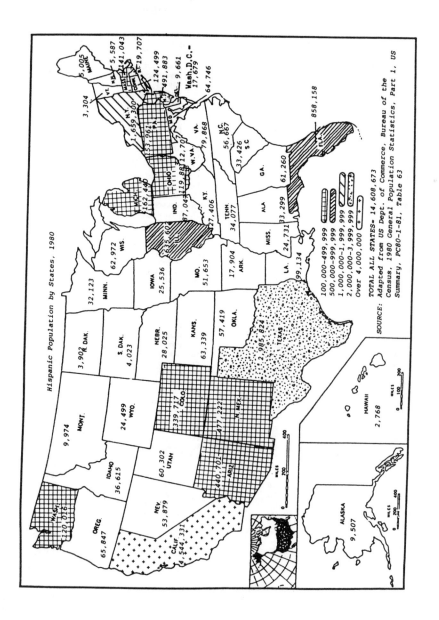

Hispanic Population by States, 1980

TOTAL ALL STATES= 14,608,673

100,000-499,999
500,000-999,999
1,000,000-1,999,999
2,000,000-3,999,999
Over 4,000,000

SOURCE: Adapted from US Dept. of Commerce, Bureau of the Census, 1980 General Population Statistics, Part 1, US Summary, PC80-1-81, Table 63

Table 14

Hispanic Population Ranked by Rural Portion of State-1980			Percent Hispanic Ranked by Rural Portion of State-1980		
Rank	State	Hispanic Population	Rank	State	Percent Hispanic
1.	Texas	416,263	1.	New Mexico	36.6%
2.	California	293,692	2.	Texas	14.4
3.	New Mexico	131,878	3.	California	14.3
4.	Arizona	59,929	4.	Arizona	13.6
5.	Colorado	51,278	5.	Colorado	9.2
6.	Florida	45,636	6.	Hawaii	8.6
7.	Washington	33,639	7.	Nevada	5.5
8.	Michigan	32,141	8.	Idaho	3.8
9.	New York	24,413	9.	Wyoming	3.3
10.	North Carolina	23,189	10.	Washington	3.1
11.	Louisiana	22,011	11.	Florida	3.0
12.	Oregon	21,224	12.	Utah	2.6
13.	Ohio	20,322	13.	Oregon	2.5
14.	Pennsylvania	16,788	14.	Louisiana	1.7
15.	Georgia	16,766	15.	New Jersey	1.6
16.	Idaho	16,498	16.	Alaska	1.3
17.	Illinois	15,907	17.	Kansas	1.3
18.	South Carolina	13,587	18.	Oklahoma	1.2
19.	Virginia	13,267	19.	Michigan	1.2
20.	New Jersey	12,826	20.	Delaware	1.1
21.	Alabama	12,405	21.	Nebraska	1.0
22.	Oklahoma	12,366	22.	South Carolina	0.9
23.	Mississippi	12,353	23.	Mississippi	0.9
24.	Kentucky	12,244	24.	New York	0.9
25.	Tennessee	11,863	25.	Connecticut	0.9
26.	Hawaii	11,181	26.	Montana	0.9
27.	Indiana	10,712	27.	Illinois	0.8
28.	Kansas	10,279	28.	Georgia	0.8
29.	Missouri	8,482	29.	Alabama	0.8
30.	Wisconsin	8,390	30.	North Carolina	0.8
31.	West Virginia	8,131	31.	Virginia	0.7
32.	Arkansas	7,789	32.	Ohio	0.7
33.	Massachusetts	6,445	33.	Arkansas	0.7
34.	Nevada	6,430	34.	Massachusetts	0.7
35.	Utah	5,909	35.	Maryland	0.7
36.	Connecticut	5,814	36.	Kentucky	0.7
37.	Wyoming	5,792	37.	West Virginia	0.7
38.	Maryland	5,695	38.	Tennessee	0.7
39.	Nebraska	5,634	39.	Indiana	0.5
40.	Minnesota	5,038	40.	Missouri	0.5
41.	Iowa	4,687	41.	Rhode Island	0.5
42.	Montana	3,158	42.	Vermont	0.5
43.	Maine	2,120	43.	Wisconsin	0.5
44.	Alaska	1,893	44.	Pennsylvania	0.5
45.	Delaware	1,863	45.	New Hampshire	0.4
46.	New Hampshire	1,806	46.	Iowa	0.4
47.	Vermont	1,718	47.	South Dakota	0.4
48.	South Dakota	1,436	48.	North Dakota	0.4
49.	North Dakota	1,265	49.	Minnesota	0.4
50.	Rhode Island	656	50.	Maine	0.4
51.	Dist. of Col.	0	51.	Dist. of Col.	0.0
Total		1,474,808	Total		2.5%

Source: U.S. Bureau of the Census, 1980 Census of Population, General Population Characteristics, PC80-1-B1, Tables 62 and 63.

Table 15

1980 Total Population		Black Population	
Top 50 Cities		Top 50 Cities	
1 New York, NY	7,071,639	1 New York, NY	1,788,377
2 Chicago, IL	3,005,078	2 Chicago, IL	1,197,174
3 Los Angeles, CA	2,966,850	3 Detroit, MI	758,468
4 Philadelphia, PA	1,688,210	4 Philadelphia, PA	638,788
5 Houston, TX	1,595,167	5 Los Angeles, CA	504,301
6 Detroit, MI	1,203,339	6 Washington, DC	448,370
7 Dallas, TX	904,074	7 Houston, TX	439,604
8 San Diego, CA	875,538	8 Baltimore, MD	430,934
9 Phoenix, AZ	789,704	9 New Orleans, LA	308,039
10 Baltimore, MD	786,775	10 Memphis, TN	307,573
11 San Antonio, TX	785,809	11 Atlanta, GA	283,158
12 Indianapolis, IN	700,719	12 Dallas, TX	265,105
13 San Francisco, CA	678,974	13 Cleveland, OH	251,084
14 Memphis, TN	646,356	14 St. Louis, MO	206,170
15 Washington, DC	638,333	15 Newark, NJ	191,968
16 Milwaukee, WI	636,212	16 Oakland, CA	159,351
17 San Jose, CA	629,442	17 Birmingham, AL	158,200
18 Cleveland, OH	573,822	18 Indianapolis, IN	152,590
19 Columbus, OH	564,866	19 Milwaukee, WI	147,055
20 Boston, MA	562,994	20 Jacksonville, FL	137,150
21 New Orleans, LA	557,515	21 Cincinnati, OH	130,490
22 Jacksonville, FL	540,920	22 Boston, MA	126,438
23 Seattle, WA	493,846	23 Columbus, OH	124,689
24 Denver, CO	492,365	24 Kansas City, MO	122,336
25 Nashville-Davidson, TN	455,663	25 Richmond, VA	112,426
26 St. Louis, MO	453,085	26 Gary, IN	107,539
27 Kansas City, MO	448,154	27 Nashville-Davidson, TN	105,869
28 El Paso, TX	425,259	28 Pittsburgh, PA	101,549
29 Atlanta, GA	425,022	29 Charlotte, NC	97,896
30 Pittsburgh, PA	423,938	30 Buffalo, NY	95,622
31 Oklahoma City, OK	403,243	31 Jackson, MS	95,218
32 Cincinnati, OH	385,457	32 Norfolk, VA	93,977
33 Fort Worth, TX	385,166	33 Fort Worth, TX	87,635
34 Minneapolis, MN	370,951	34 Miami, FL	87,018
35 Portland, OR	366,423	35 San Francisco, CA	86,190
36 Honolulu (CDP), HI	365,048	36 Shreveport, LA	84,691
37 Long Beach, CA	361,334	37 Louisville, KY	84,254
38 Tulsa, OK	360,919	38 Baton Rouge, LA	79,848
39 Buffalo, NY	357,870	39 San Diego, CA	77,508
40 Toledo, OH	354,635	40 Dayton, OH	75,136
41 Miami, FL	346,865	41 Mobile, AL	72,697
42 Austin, TX	345,544	42 Montgomery, AL	69,821
43 Oakland, CA	339,337	43 Savanna, GA	69,265
44 Alburquerque, NM	331,767	44 Flint, MI	66,060
45 Tucson, AZ	330,537	45 East Orange, NJ	64,650
46 Newark, NJ	329,248	46 Tampa, FL	63,578
47 Charlotte, NC	314,447	47 Rochester, NY	62,256
48 Omaha, NE	314,267	48 Jersey City, NJ	61,957
49 Louisville, KY	298,455	49 Toledo, OH	61,855
50 Birmingham, AL	284,413	50 Compton, CA	60,874

Source: American Demographics

Table 16

Percent Black Population	Hispanic Population

Top 50 Cities		Top 50 Cities	
1 East St. Louis, IL	95.6%	1 New York, NY	1,406,389
2 East Orange, NJ	83.2	2 Los Angeles, CA	815,305
3 Compton, CA	74.9	3 Chicago, IL	423,357
4 Gary, IN	70.8	4 San Antonio, TX	421,808
5 Washington, DC	70.2	5 Houston, TX	280,691
6 Atlanta, GA	66.6	6 El Paso, TX	265,997
7 Detroit, MI	63.0	7 Miami, FL	194,185
8 Newark, NJ	58.3	8 San Jose, CA	140,318
9 Inglewood,CA	57.3	9 San Diego, CA	129,953
10 Birmingham, AL	55.6	10 Phoenix, AZ	116,875
11 New Orleans, LA	55.3	11 Albuquerque, NM	112,030
12 Baltimore, MD	54.8	12 Dallas, TX	110,511
13 Camden, NJ	53.0	13 Corpus Christi, TX	108,229
14 Richmond, VA	51.3	14 Hialeah, FL	107,889
15 Wilmington, DE	51.2	15 E. Los Angeles(CDP), CA	103,514
16 Pine Bluff, AR	49.1	16 Denver, CO	92,257
17 Savannah, GA	49.0	17 Santa Ana, GA	90,652
18 Monroe, LA	48.6	18 Laredo, TX	85,057
19 Mount Vernon, NY	48.4	19 San Francisco, CA	84,194
20 Richmond, CA	47.9	20 Tucson, AZ	82,106
21 Alexandria, LA	47.8	21 Brownsville, TX	71,215
22 Memphis, TN	47.6	22 Austin, TX	64,945
23 Albany, GA	47.5	23 Philadelphia, PA	64,323
24 Durham, NC	47.1	24 Newark, NJ	61,322
25 Oakland, CA	47.0	25 Fresno, CA	51,271
26 Jackson, MS	46.9	26 Long Beach, CA	50,450
27 Charleston, SC	46.6	27 El Monte, CA	48,704
28 St. Louis, MO	45.5	28 Fort Worth, TX	48,568
29 Trenton, NJ	45.4	29 Oxnard, CA	47,970
30 Portsmouth, VA	45.1	30 McAllen, TX	47,395
31 Macon, GA	44.5	31 Jersey City, NJ	41,757
32 Cleveland, OH	43.8	32 Pico Rivera, CA	40,705
33 Harrisburg, PA	43.6	33 Paterson, NJ	39,551
34 Flint, MI	41.4	34 South Gate, CA	38,951
35 Shreveport, LA	41.2	35 Sacramento, CA	38,905
36 Fayetteville, NC	40.9	36 Anaheim, CA	37,591
37 Port Arthur, TX	40.6	37 Boston, MA	36,430
38 Columbia, SC	40.3	38 Pueblo, CO	36,060
39 Winston-Salem, NC	40.2	39 Tampa, FL	35,781
40 Chicago, IL	39.8	40 Union City, NJ	35,562
41 Montgomery, AL	39.3	41 Norwalk, CA	34,214
42 Irvington, NJ	38.1	42 Stockton, CA	33,151
43 Lake Charles, LA	38.0	43 Lubbock, TX	32,667
44 Philadelphia, PA	37.8	44 Oakland, CA	32,133
45 Pontiac, MI	37.1	45 Montebello, CA	31,296
46 Dayton, OH	36.9	46 Salinas, CA	30,577
47 Beaumont, TX	36.6	47 San Bernardino, CA	29,820
48 Baton Rouge, LA	36.4	48 Baldwin Park, CA	29,336
49 Mobile, AL	36.3	49 Detroit, MI	28,466
50 Greenville, SC	35.6	50 Pomona, CA	28,302

Source: American Demographics

Table 17

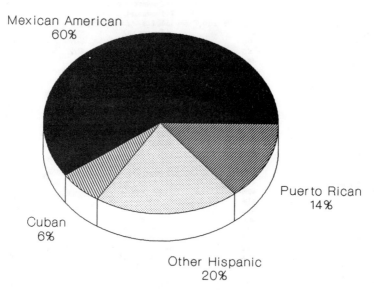

Distribution of Hispanic Population
in the U.S., by source of Origin: 1980

Mexican American
60%

Puerto Rican
14%

Cuban
6%

Other Hispanic
20%

Source: US. Bureau of the Census, 1981.
"Persons of Spanish Origin by State:
1980".

Table 18

TOP NINE STATES IN HISPANIC POPULATION: 1980
(States with 250,000 or more Hispanics)

State	Rank	Number of Hispanics	Percent distribution
U.S. total	- -	14,608,673	100.00
California	1	4,544,331	31.1
Texas	2	2,985,824	20.4
New York	3	1,659,300	11.4
Florida	4	858,158	5.9
Illinois	5	635,602	4.4
New Jersey	6	491,883	3.4
New Mexico	7	477,222	3.3
Arizona	8	440,701	3.0
Colorado	9	339,717	2.3
Total in nine top states		12,432,738	85.1

Source: U.S. Bureau of the Census. "Persons of Spanish Origin by state: 1980." *1980 Census of Population. Supplementary Report* PC80-S1-7.

"While Hispanics reside in every state of the union five states contain almost 75 percent of all Hispanics in the U.S. Hispanics like Blacks are highly urbanized: 83 percent live in metropolitan areas, versus 77 percent of Blacks and 66 percent Whites. Close to half of all Hispanics (48 percent) live within ten Metropolitan areas; Los Angeles contains more than two million Hispanics, and New York over 1.5 million. California and Texas, plus the metroplitan areas of New York, Miami and Chicago, account for 70 percent of the Hispanic population." *Hispanics: Challenges and Opportunities.* A working paper from the Ford Foundation p. 21 and 22, 1984.

How do we recruit them?

Early identification is paramount to the success of effective recruiting efforts.

Some Universities use what they call a "cultivation plan". Different representatives from the various departments are assigned different schools across the state in order to develop more personal relationships with students to increase enrollment.

A university in Virginia split up its admission application making it easier for students to fill out. The result was many more students applied. Some campuses find that currently enrolled students make excellent recruiters. Others involve the faculty.

Princeton sponsors a (Minority Week) similar to 'Discover Dartmouth' to attract minority students trying to decide between Princeton and another school.

Some campuses conduct phone-a-thons and direct mail marketing campaigns to individual students, families and minority community based organizations.

Some Universities set laudable goals. For example, Louisiana State University wants its Black student enrollment to reflect a "real world balance" and according to one of its recruiters by 1988 planned to have a Black student enrollment of approximately 18%.

Minority organizations are trying out creative approaches as well. A member of the Arizona Association of Chicanos for Higher Education (AACHE) advised AACHE members to train other Chicanos to replace them at a three to one ratio.

After your applicant pool has been identified the principal barrier to access to higher education is a financial one. There was little disagreement from the research that financial aid was the most important factor in recruiting minority students.

Minority family median income is still less than that of Whites (see table 23). The inability to pay for a college education often determines whether individuals will pursue a postsecondary education or not. It may also determine a student's choice of a four year institution or a junior college. This choice is significant in that a disproportionate number of minority students are enrolled in two year institutions where the attrition rate is higher. This path looms as a dangerous one to the baccalaureate degree.

A failure to provide adequate resources for minority students can be just as effective in a discriminatory fashion as denying admission based on race. So no matter how "progressive" an institution's admission policy might be, if it fails to provide students with adequate funding to attend then it may be denying students opportunities based on both class and race.

Several Ivy League institutions practice a "need blind" admissions policy in which applications are considered for admission regardless of their need for financial aid. Accepted applicants are then given 100 percent of the money they need, as determined by the financial aid office, in the form of grants, loans, scholarships and employment.

Other campuses have launched multi-million dollar scholarship campaigns. They use the interest to supplement students' financial aids. Still others have established an endowment for the recruitment and enrollment of minority students.

With dwindling financial resources on the national level the issue of access threatens to widen the gulf between White and Minority students. Add to this the shocking increase in tuition fees nationally and the reduction in grants by philanthropic agencies and the real threat to minority educational gains becomes apparent. For the forseeable future the civil rights struggle may prove to be an economic one that if left unresolved threatens to exacerbate class divisions in the society.

Clearly money is of paramount importance. But even if students had adequate resources to attend the University of their choice there are other factors involved as well.

Institutions recruit students to the total environment of their communities. Whether minority students experience hassels in obtaining housing, suspicious stares from merchants while shopping, intimidation by campus and city police or suffer an inadequate social life helps in determining where they will attend college. The reputation of an institution's professors and commitment to ensuring a comfortable, accepting environment on the part of campus adminstrators are also important factors.

Over the past 20 years many campuses have created positions for minority recruiters, who serve as role models, have   an understanding of minority student concerns and help students prepare for a new environment.

"Information is the key to good recruitment," says Robert Brown III, a former recruiter at the University of Wisconsin-Madison. *"Students should be honestly informed about the community, the school and told about the resources that are available to assist them".*

Our findings tend to support Mr. Brown's statement. Additionally, we found that the personal contact approach by recruiters yielded the best results. Meetings with high school counselors and students are still considered some of the best recruitment practices. Unfortunately, due to cost considerations, recruiters are becoming increasingly less able to meet with potential students. To combat this loss of personal contact, minority admissions representatives are organizing to work together in an effort to improve minority enrollment and retention at their respective institutions. An excellent example of this is the New England Consortium of Black Admissions Counselors (NECBAC).

It's membership includes over thirty institutions in

the New England area. It is chartered as a non-profit organization and provides valuable information and resources to its members.

Combining efforts provides benefits in terms of dispersing information as well as helping to eliminate competition between schools and states for a limited number of students.

What things do we consider before we admit them?

Since the Bakke and Adam court cases many universities concerned with questions pertaining to special admission practices have been following guidelines similar to the ones listed below.

They are:

A. Race and/or ethnic background can be considered as a factor for admission.

B. Minority applicants should be reviewed on an individual basis rather than on a group basis for admission purposes.

C. Although quotas are not allowed, universities can use numerical goals and timetables.

D. Separate admission programs are unacceptable.

E. Test scores should not be used exclusively to determine admission.

It has been suggested that the Adams case tended to show a trend for proportional representation of Minority groups. This has special significance for states with large Minority groups.   Some significant highlights from this case are:

A. Requiring state-wide coordinated plans rather than individual institutional plans.

B. Encouraging aggressive Affirmative Action which goes beyond removal of barriers to actual access.

C. Requiring states to strive for parity of enrollment.

D. Requiring universities to strive for parity of retention and progress from matriculation to graduation.

Other Considerations

Sedlecek (1977) and Burlew (1979) found that non-academic indicators can be used to predict educational attainment among black youth. Non-academic predictors considered important in their study included ability to establish long range goals, successful leadership experiences, self perceptions, and community service. Other researchers suggest that admission personnel include such variables as self concept, ambition, and maturity as a means of predicting academic success.

According to Davis (1970) Oberlin admitted blacks for a while based on their "hipness". This concept includes competitiveness, high motivation and self reliance. A study was conducted to ascertain the effect of such an unusual admission's practice. A total of three groups were admitted; 18 were not "hip" but met regular criteria; 14 were both "hip" and met regular criteria; and seven were "hip" but did not meet regular criteria. At the end of the first semester, there was no appreciable difference in the distribution of grade point averages between the three groups.

Creative admission approaches challenge the widely held belief that standards are lowered when campuses award different treatment in letting students enter an institution. Some educators argue that minority students bring to campuses talents and experiences that often go unrecognized in the traditional admissions process, and even though many enter with lower S.A.T. scores they're able to compete and achieve on a par with the majority population. They ask for special attention in getting in - not in the classroom.

The debate rages in the literature among educators concerning how successful standardized tests and high school grades are in predicting academic success. Pouring more fuel to the fire, author David Owen in his book, *None of the Above* says the S.A.T. is no better than chance at predicting a student's college success adding that *"preparatory courses can improve standardized test scores by as much as 200 points,"* (Owen, 1985).

Researchers at the University of Michigan's Reading and Learning Skills Center found that both the S.A.T. and high school rank were "worse than chance" at predicting whether student athletes would graduate.

Yet campuses continue to use standardized tests, in part, to base their decisions whether to admit or not to admit a potential student.

Additional Concerns

"An alarming trend emerging in some of the elite universities is the policy of selecting Black students who are graduates of primarily white high schools. The highly selective admissions policies which seek not only the highest achievers but also those who have been socialized in white environments can result in the development of an elite Black leadership class who will not identify with and will have little sympathy for the problems of the Black poor, thus widening the chasm between Black middle class and Black lower class." (Smith, 1980).

This is a legitimate concern that could easily contribute to the creation of an underclass if not consciously fought. It takes little imagination to predict the concentration of low income Black and Hispanic students in community colleges and similar inexpensive schools which offer limited programs and some of questionable quality. This represents a dilemma that can only be resolved by universities adopting admission criteria that reaches a fair balance between academic and non-academic variables, by making college affordable and providing the funds and support necessary for students to matriculate.

The high concentration of minority students in junior colleges poses both problems and opportunities. The problems (higher attrition rates, limited program choices, etc.), have been mentioned. The opportunities are emerging somewhat slower.

The College Board publishes a *Talent Roster* of *Outstanding Minority Community College Graduates*. In 1985 a total of 2,186 students were selected from nominations submitted by 265 community colleges throughout the nation. The Talent Roster serves as a valuable resource to four-year colleges in identifying promising minority transfer students and has assisted many students in gaining admission and scholarships to four year institutions.

UCLA has initiated a pilot project with eight Los Angeles County community colleges to promote the continuity of course offerings between the colleges and UCLA and to improve academic preparation for potential transfer students.

To participate, the colleges must agree to offer the necessary courses to satisfy UCLA requirements, to develop a "college-within-a-college" program promoting faculty mentorship, to appoint an academic adviser to develop and monitor a transfer plan for each student, to participate in program assessment and research procedures, and to participate in faculty-to-faculty exchanges on comparability of course content and rigor. The ultimate winners may be the students if they find a smooth transition from the community college to UCLA.

In closing out this section on recruitment and admissions its important to keep in mind that significant changes have occurred in minority student college attendance patterns in the U.S. over the past two decades. Prior to 1964,

60 percent of Black students attended historically Black institutions, but by 1973 the proportion had declined to roughly 25 percent. Until 1968 nearly 80 percent of all undergraduate degrees awarded to Blacks were earned at Black colleges and universities, (Gurin and Epps, 1975).

In contrast,

by 1978-79 an estimated 56 percent of all bachelor's degrees awarded to Black students were conferred by predominantly White schools, (Deskins, 1981).

The implications of this social phenomena need to be analyzed in depth. On the surface this suggests that pre-dominantly white schools are enrolling minorities in great numbers. However when you consider there are over 3,000 predominantly white institutions compared to the 117 predomi-nantly black institutions, these figures become less impressive. Tables 19-21 provide enrollment information in greater detail.

Table 19

	Enrollment Since 1980 and Two Year Changes		
	1980	1982	1984
American Indian	84,000	88,000	83,000
Asian	286,000	351,000	382,000
Black	1,107,000	1,101,000	1,070,000
Hispanic	472,000	519,000	529,000
White	9,833,000	9,997,000	9,767,000

Figures have been rounded to nearest thousand
Source: U.S. Department of Education

Table 20

Percentage 1984 Enrollment by Type of Institution				
Public	American Indian	Asian	Black	Hispanic	White
Universities	12.7	17.1	9.3	9.2	18.6
Other 4-year	23.0	23.5	30.4	23.9	24.5
2-year	50.9	42.5	39.0	52.5	34.0
Private					
Universities	2.4	7.3	4.0	4.1	6.0
Other 4 year	7.2	8.9	13.6	8.5	15.0
2-year	3.8	0.7	3.7	1.8	1.9

Table 21

1984 Enrollment by Class Ranking				
	American Indian	Asian	Black	Hispanic	White
Undergraduate	0.7	3.2	9.5	4.6	79.9
Graduate	0.3	2.6	4.8	2.2	80.2
Professional	0.4	3.3	4.8	2.9	87.4
Unclassified	0.7	3.2	8.0	4.5	82.0

Source: U.S. Department of Education

Recruitment and Admissions Initiatives

Consider developing a state systemwide newsletter and disseminating it to minority students beginning in middle school, providing information about various campuses and about courses they need in high school to prepare for college. A systemwide approach allows the costs to be spread among several campuses with potential benefits for all campuses involved. Some Campuses have experienced success with one or more of the following approaches:

- Developed a *Preparation for College* pamphlet for prospective middle and high school students.

- Produced a series of video tapes for dissemination in high schools that emphasize faculty excellence.

- Involved Minority students currently enrolled on campus in their recruitment efforts.

- Required each school or department to work with the office of admissions in developing and implementing minority recruitment plans.

- Used national search lists.

- Developed a coordinated plan for telephone recruiting.

- Used regional pre-college program networks.

- Established linkages with existing local, state and national Minority networks.

- Involved middle and high school teachers with the indentification process. Too often this group is ignored.

Innovative Recruitment and Admissions Programs
(taken from Campus press releases and student newspapers)

Hispanic Admissions

The Center for Chicano-Boricua Studies (CCBS) is

a higher education access program for Hispanics in Michigan. Through the program, Hispanics can be given special admission to Wayne State University and can take their first year of classes through the Center, along with general requirements. These services allow students to function on a college level and prepare them for second-year mainstreaming. CCBS is presently conducting research to determine if there is a difference in retention and dropout rates by subgroups of Hispanics involved in the program. These Hispanics can be broadly defined as Cubans, Central Americans, Chicanos (Mexicans) and Puerto Ricans. The research data would then help focus the efforts in needed areas.

Recruiting Endowment Fund

Louisiana State University (LSU) is considering an endowment for the recruitment and enrollment of minority Students. Suggestions have been made to contact the top 100 to 200 minorities in the state. LSU is combining its efforts with other departments to establish a working solution on how minority students can be recruited and retained on campus. The nine-member council wants this year to be a big year for recruiting minorities and would like to see an endowment incorporated into the University's budget or received from private funding.

Phone-A-Thon

Penn State sponsored a phone-a-thon to get more black students to apply at the University and increase Black enrollment. The phone-a-thon gives prospective minority students a chance to ask enrolled minority students about the University. Most of the questions are of a general nature on admissions and financial aid. Also, by calling early it is hoped that will encourage students to apply early for financial aid and admission purposes.

Minority Recruitment Conference

In an effort to encourage more people to obtain a graduate education in professions which directly impact minority groups, the University of Conneticut's School of Social Work held a Minority Recruitment Conference. The conference provided information on the various subject area specialization available-including casework, administration, policy and planning etc. Admission requirements, deadlines, procedures and availability of financial aids were discussed.

Hispanic Recruiting

The College Recruitment Association for Hispanics (CRAH) familiarizes parents and potential students about educational opportunities in Michigan. CRAH is an organization made up of Admission's counselors from several Michigan Colleges and Universities.

Recruitment and Admission Resources

ABAFAOILSS - The Association of Black Admissions & Financial Aid Offices of the Ivy League and Sister Schools
c/o Doris Davis
Yale University
P.O. Box 1502A
Yale Station
New Haven, CT 06520   203/432-1916

Office of Minority Concerns
American Council on Education
1 Dupont Circle, NW
Washington, DC 20036
Publishes an "Annual Status Report on Minorities in Higher Education", which contains a wealth of statistics detailing the participation at all levels of higher education. Costs $5 and must be prepaid.

National Association for the Advancement of Blacks
in Vocational Education
3476 Renault St.
Memphis, TN 38118 901/362-8654

New England Consortium of Black Admissions Counselors
P.O. Box 1383
Waltham, MA 02254

American Association of Collegiate Registars and Admissions
Officers (AACRAO)
One Dupont Circle NW, Suite 330
Washington, DC 20036   202/293-9161

American College Testing Program (ACT)
2201 North Dodge Street, P.O. Box 168
Iowa City, IA 52243

College Entrance Examination Board (CEEB)
888 Seventh Ave.
New York, NY 10106

National Action Council for Minorities in Engineering
3 West 35th Street
New York, NY 10001 212/279-2626

MATRICULATION

There are three sets of figures admission personnel should monitor. The number of minority student contacted, the number admitted and the actual number that show. It is the last figure that determines whether one's matriculation efforts are effective. If twenty-five new minority freshmen are admitted to your institution and only four show, you have a problem.

While it may not be realistic to expect that all students admitted will attend a particular institution, it would be counter productive not to make some special efforts to increase one's show rate.

A personal telephone call and letter to the potential student and his/her parents are quite effective. Inviting the student to campus and providing access to campus facilities is a solid strategy.

The personal attention paid to prospective students during this critical juncture can spell the difference in whether they attend or not. Getting the student to say "I'm coming" is only the first step however. An effective matriculation program ensures that each newly admitted student receives proper advising enabling him/her to enroll in appropriate classes. Students are informed when orientation activities occur as well as informed about support services available to assist them. Matriculation services involve monitoring of placement and diagnostic tests, financial aid and housing follow up.

Some institutions provide an orientation to the non-collegiate community recognizing that students will spend a great deal of time out in the community.

The matriculation component is the link in the retention chain that often gets ignored. It is generally assumed that during registration week students will get the assistance they need to begin their academic journey. What usually happens is that new students are locked out of preferred courses and end up with scheduling nightmares. Emphasizing matriculation activities is like dotting i's and crossing t's. Most importantly it lays the foundation for a smooth orientation to college.

RETENTION ISSUES

Dr. Rodolfo Cortina's (chair of the task force which studied the Wisconsin system's record of recruiting and retaining minority students) report says the issue is no longer access but retention which he characterizes as a "revolving door". This indicates a shift from access to the ability of minority students to persist.

Nationwide, minority student retention is still less than that of white students. A Ford Foundation study (reported in the *Chronicle of Higher Education,* Feb 3, 1982) points out, that nationally only about 42% of minority students entering college go on to complete their degrees while approximately 60% of white students do so. A minimum goal would be to have the retention rates for minority students the same as those for non-minority students.

Research on student retention nationally identifies three major factors related to dropping out of school: I) academic preparation, II) socio-cultural adjustment, and III) financial resources.

I. Academic Preparation

America's schools are failing its minorities and its poor. This failure is explained in the literature from three different but interrelated perspectives:

1) Societal causes that have deep historical roots,

2) Institutional causes that have been internally adopted by a school or school system that results in negative outcomes and unequal conditions for Minorities, and

3) Individual causes attributed to the learner.

1) Societal causes explaining the poor academic preparation minority students receive.

Proponents of this view argue that remedies lie outside educational structures and require massive shifts in

the power, resources and cultural practices of the society for
any lasting benefits to occur.

The issue of academic failure by minority groups, can
be characterized under this view as, *"methodical, ideological,
permanent, and an essential element in the way the whole society
is organized and it is racial,"*(Hilliard, 1978).

This suggests that a different method is needed for
looking at the problem.

> Present human relations theory, multicultural theory, cultural
> pluralism theory, bilingual theory, race relations theory, cultural deprivation
> theory...are all devoid of a theory for the origins of oppression, (Ibid, p.4).

Hillard calls for a systematic study of the history of
education under colonization resulting in a model for examin-
ing education under oppression.

The work of Frantz Fanon *Black Skin, White Masks; A
Dying Colonialism* and Albert Memmi's book *Colonizer and the
Colonized* support this view.

A book by John Hodge, called *Cultural Bases for
Racism and Group Oppression: An Examination of Traditional
"Western" Concepts, Values and Institutional Structures Which
Support Racism, Sexism and Elitism* offers a good analysis of
some of the assumptions that almost by themselves will guarantee that we participate knowingly or unknowingly in op-
pressive actions thus perpetuating inequitable conditions.
Alan Chase's book called *The Legacy of Malthus* documents
how the current system of oppression was created.

Carter Woodson's book called *The Miseducation of the
Negro* chronicles how the educational system wasn't designed
to produce equality but dependency.

> The colonial situation [imposed on Minority groups] depends upon
> a system that maintains privilege, profit and use of patient for the colonizer",
> (Hilliard,1978).

Citing an example of what it would mean to educate Blacks in South Africa.

It would change the politics of South Africa overnight. So consequently, you must have scholarly rationales of why that can't happen. That's why you have as much IQ testing going on in South Africa as you do here. Standardized testing is big business in South Africa...The same ones that we use, (Ibid, p. 13).

Hillard's colonial model is offered as a conceptual map for looking at the entire system of oppression in education and how that contributes to black and minority student failure.

Another major theme supported by our research as a major cause resulting in inequity is the nature of the capitalistic system itself. The neo-Marxist approach to education according to Spring, (1982) claims that,

The problem with the present educational system in the U.S. is that its policies and actions are controlled by big business. The goal of big business is to use the school system to teach a capitalistic ideology designed to get the student to accept inequalities in society. Thus the schools are designed to perpetuate social class differences, (Ibid, p.23).

Carnoy, (1983) believes,

Our society continues to have an undemocratic system of production, and the inequalities and hierarchies of that system profoundly shape all other institutions, including education, (Ibid, p. 401).

Bowles (1972) contends that the educational system merely acts to translate social classes into occupational status.

...our schools have evolved not as a part of a pursuit of equality but rather to meet the needs of capitalistic employers for a disciplined and skilled labor force and to provide a mechanism for social control in the interest of political stability (Ibid, p.43).

Ogbu says this results in a caste like state for minorities.

Under this dual system...no amount of educational reform and no programs to rehabilitate members of the caste like minorities can bring about equal school performance by the two groups, (Ogbu, 1978).

This theme of oppression, capitalism and inequality is repeated throughout the literature (Silberman, 1971; Anderson, 1972; Hilliard, 1978; Levin, 1982; Spring, 1982 and Komoski, 1983).

U.S. society is characterized as a highly unequal place in terms of income distribution, material deprivation, economic and political power.

The literature tends to paint a pessimistic picture of achieving equity and thus improved academic preparation under the present economic system.

Given this preoccupation by the literature, improved performance gains by minority groups can only come about through structural and fundamental change in the economic system of the society.

Ogbu would argue that the principle cause of Black academic retardation is that the schools translate the inferior social and technoeconomic status of Blacks into inferior education.

...that caste barriers do not permit Blacks to translate their academic skills into good jobs, income and other benefits", (Ogbu, 1978, p. 357).

He maintains that the elimination of caste barriers is the only *"lasting solution to the problem of academic retardation,"*(Ibid, p. 357).

2) Institutional causes of inequity that have been internally adopted by a school or school system that results in negative outcomes and unequal conditions for minorities based on racism, class, and related barriers that the school itself has created.

This approach suggests that remedies might be found by

analyzing school practices and pedagogical methods. It acknowledges that societal factors influencing income, class
status, etc., will still present obstacles but within the school
itself a more equitable environment can be created.

What may be needed is a better understanding by
teachers that they wield considerable control of "within"
school factors. Analyzing these factors (such as tracking,
grouping, teachers expectation, etc.), may help teachers
decide whether changes in school practices and pedogogical
methods are needed thus improving performance.

Teachers' expectations are cited by the literature as
contributing to inequity Dusek (1975) and Banks (1981).
Teacher training is also identified by the literature as contributing to unequal conditions in the classroom. It appears that
most teachers are middle-class or have a middle class orientation while a disproportionate number of minority students are
poor or lower class.

> The clash of cultures in the classroom is essentially a class war, a
> socio-economic and racial warfare being waged on the battle ground of our
> schools with middle class teachers provided with a powerful arsenal of
> half truths, prejudices and rationalizations arrayed against hopelessly out-
> classed working class youngsters. This is an uneven balance, particularly
> since, like most battles, it comes under the guise of righteousness, (Clark,
> 1965).

Current practices in teacher training need to be
evaluated. Crim, (1970) noted that problems facing teacher
training for [Minorities] include language barriers, cultural
gaps and teacher career patterns.

Although the literature is unclear as to a preferred
pedagogical approach that would enhance equal opportunities,
it does make clear the need for new pedagogical approaches.

3) Individual Causes of Inequity Attributed to the Learner

This approach puts the burden of learning and

achievement on the learner. It is characterized as "blaming the victim" by some, (Hilliard, 1978).

The reason for minority student failure and social conditions is explained in part because of a lack of motivation on the part of individuals, their families or their communities. Proponents of this view, Riessman, (1962), Cutts, (1962), Larson, (1963), and Ausbuel, (1965), cite cultural deprivation theories to argue that equal opportunity is already a reality. Minority students simply need to take advantage of it. Proponents further claim that a system based on meritocracy discriminates fairly.

This approach assumes equity remedies must come from the individual or the home. Students themselves must seek out opportunities in the schools.

Although the literature suggests that in the last two decades the education of minorities has moved from remediation and physical pathology to a recognition that education itself must be reformed, there is still a strong,

> ...neoconservative dogma insisting that poor children cannot be helped in public schools and that these schools themselves cannot be improved, (Mann, 1981).

Other researchers argue that minority students' failure is linked to heredity, Jensen (1969) and (Garrett, 1971).

While the debate between environmental factors and heredity (in explaining minority student failure) is still being waged by educators, minority youngster's schooling has benefited little by the discussion.

If new approaches are to be considered, educators, school psychologists and behaviorists must work together to meet the needs of minority student learners, but *"they must not assume that because of the economic status of minority students that they are lazy, do not want to learn or can't learn"*, (Francher, 1983).

Summary

Given this bleak assessment of the educational system, and the probability that minority students will continue to enroll in college campuses underprepared, it becomes critical for universities to respond in ways that give students a reasonable chance to succeed in college.

The general response by campuses has been to establish remedial programs. Learning centers, tutorial labs, specialized courses and a variety of academic activities have been tried, some meeting with greater success than others.

A persuasive case has already been built for remedial education. The research shows that the absence of academic support programs may make even the most promising minority students academic casualties unnecessarily. There is a substantial body of research that links the lack of remedial services to high attrition rates.

Many educators argue it is not the role of institutions of higher learning to provide remedial education. They say that if students can't "cut the mustard" they shouldn't be there, adding that resources used to provide such services could be better allocated elsewhere.

This view although popular is short sighted. Further it ignores the reasons why remedial education is necessary. To deny minority students additional help once they reach the college ranks is to punish them twice, to limit their life choices, and to exonerate the institutions that prepared them.

We don't believe the argument that the money could be better spent elsewhere is a strong one either. Society pays for its poorly educated through higher welfare costs, the criminal justice system, unemployment payments, etc. It makes better sense to intervene early on. While it is certainly preferred that this intervention occur in elementary and middle school, it is irresponsible for universities and colleges to wipe their hands of this crisis having contributed to its existence.

II. Socio-Cultural Adjustment

Although this issue is discussed in greater detail in Chapter 4, we believe it is important to briefly comment on it as it impacts retention.

Dr. Jacqueline Fleming's study confirms that the social environment of the campus affects the academic performances of the student, (Fleming, 1984). For any retention program to be successful, it must address socio-cultural adjustment type problems minority students encounter on predominantly white campuses.

Perhaps there is no greater feeling of alienation than to believe that one has to "go it alone". Such feelings may lead to high attrition rates.

III. Financial Resources

Tuition levels and enrollment rates are related. In a study on "The Effect of Tuition and Financial Aid on Access and Choice in Postsecondary Education" it was found that a $100 tuition decrease would produce an average 3 percent enrollment rate increase.

Discriminatory tuition changes favoring low-income students would raise enrollment rates more than would general reductions.

Research has revealed several general conclusions about financial aid; many students could not attend college without aid, grants raise enrollment rates more than do loans or work-study programs; increased aid may have less effect on enrollment and may produce a different student composition than would tuition changes and offering aid affects the student's decision on where to apply, where as the dollar amount of aid offered affects his choice of institution (Hyde, 1978).

What may be needed are sound financial aid practices that take into consideration the high need that some students enter college with. Financial aid offices have the flexibilty to structure guidelines so that students with the highest financial needs can be met. The mix of loan and grant amounts that students receive pose serious consequences because a pattern is emerging nationally in which minority students are graduating with nearly twice the loan debt of white students. To enter and leave college at a disadvantage is a unfair burden for minority students to bear.

Other Factors Associated With Retention

Successful progammatic responses to retention problems address the factors that create the problems. Some campuses do this by conducting a policy review to evaluate how policies affect students along racial lines. Policies that are applied equally are not always applied fairly. A review of what minority students are majoring in, provides clues as to the type of academic advice students are given. A check to see how minority students are utilizing campus services would also prove revealing. Whether or not texts used are multicultural,the staff is multicultural, campus committees are multicultural, pictures displayed on the walls (environment) throughout the campus are multicultural, all contribute to retention efforts.

UCLA found (in its preparatory program) that if it revamped its orientation and student outreach programs and increased the funding allocated to these efforts, a significant drop in the student attrition rate would occur.

They also found a personal welcome from staff, strong tutorial assistance and targeting the freshmen class produced the best results.

At Valencia Community College in Orlando Florida campus planners found out many Black students failed to return to college because of perceived lack of support and outreach efforts. Programs stressing Black awareness and workshops on study skills and test anxiety were among the support services most desired by Black students.

The University of Texas's Dean of Student office matches faculty mentors with minority students in an effort to increase minority student retention. A few campuses have created full time retention coordinator positions.

Summary

Minority student retention must be viewed as a total college effort involving all aspects of the institution. After all, there is already in place a supportive and holistic environment for white students.

Retention efforts represent the foundation of an institution's total efforts. They include programmatic activities, Orientation, The Freshman Year, Academic Advising, Counseling, Learning Resources, Faculty Involvement, and Student Incentives. We'll speak to each of these areas next.

There is little disagreement in the literature and from practitioners "in the field" that a good orientation program represents a vital link in the retention chain. Students in general find campuses perplexing. That's why an orientation program is critical, because it's often the first encounter a minority student has with that campus.

All students should receive an orientation to university life that will give them a feeling of belonging and a knowledge where resources and various types of assistance can be found. An orientation should be more than a superficial welcome by a detached administrator who students may never see again until graduation.

A solid orientation to college regulations and resources *"... fosters the appropriate use of helping services, which in many colleges are under utilized because students are unfamiliar with what these services offer,"* (Cohen,1978).

For an orientation to be effective and to generate the types of results that contribute to retention it should have the following characteristics:

- It informs students about what support services are available on campus and shows the importance of those services to their retention and graduation.

- It gives them an awareness of degree program requirements in their area of academic interest.

- It provides academic advising to help students complete their course scheduling.

- It familiarizes students with the process of registration.

- It discusses educational and career options.

- It provides an orientation to the non-collegiate community.

- It provides students an opportunity to interact with other students, faculty and staff.

- Through a class or seminar it stresses study skills, team building, cultural acclimation and positive self-esteem.

- It includes prior training for the majority members of institutions so that minority group students will have the opportunity to "fit in."

The University of Wisconsin-Madison's Advanced Opportunity Program has an exemplary short term orientation program. The orientation takes place over an entire week. Students are given a thorough overview on how the campus operates, who to see for a particular problem and what is required of them if their campus experience is to be successful. By the time students register for classes they not only know their way around campus, they are able to help other students who didn't receive such an orientation. The agenda for this week long orientation is impressive both in terms of substance and the objectives that guide the week long activities.

The University of South Carolina has a model orientation class which students take during their freshmen year. This classroom approach spread over an entire year has been lauded in many books and articles as reducing University of South Carolina's attrition rates.

The Black Cultural Center of Valparaiso (Indiana) has put together a helpful orientation pamphlet informing minority students of services available on campus. The booklet includes a social calendar, eleven commandments of study, tips on taking exams and a "mini-mini" survival kit. Students are encouraged to keep the booklet handy at all times as a reference when needed.

The Office of Minority Affairs at Central Michigan University sponsors an annual "get aquainted day." Faculty and students meet through day long activities that include free food, music and short speeches by college officials and minority student leaders. This informal setting gives students a chance to see faculty and staff in a different light.

Michigan State University (MSU) offers a unique program designed to aid minority students in their adjustment to the University. For those who live in the dormitories, minority aides act as an outlet to whom minority students can turn to help in adapting to MSU. The aides provide activities, social events, programs and assist with the various caucuses in the dorms.

Some schools host minority student receptions where they invite both majority and minority faculty to interact with minority students. Others hold orientation seminars periodically during the year. Many orientation programs stress the value of good class attendance, establishing new friendships, participating in campus activities and helping students to accept their opportunities and responsibilities.

A few programs we discovered try to prepare the university to receive and accommodate minority students by orientating the faculty and staff.

A former Marquette University administrator Sarah Ford used to have students participate in a mock planning exercise in which they had to interact with campus faculty and staff. For example she would give them a task to "make plans for an awards banquet honoring graduating minority students." The students would have to prepare a budget for the event, go around to the appropriate departments to reserve room space, food, etc,. They had to create an agenda for the event and make sure everything was taken care of so that the event would be successful. Through this mock activity students were able to meet faculty and staff and learned on their own, valuable lessons about planning events on campus. Students experienced both a sense of pride and accomplishment. Many claimed that this activity made their adjustment to the campus easier.

Total Campus Involvement Required

It's important that the entire university is involved in

the orientation process. This reassures students that they are a part of the total campus community. This approach also helps to reduce stigmatization by helping traditional depart-ments recognize their responsibilities in helping minority students adjust to campus.

More campuses are beginning to realize that effective orientation programs are just as important for new graduate students as it is for undergraduate students. While these orien-tation programs include many of the characteristics described previously, they also provide information about the process of earning a masters or Ph D. Students are introduced to re-search methods, computer searches and shown how to locate information in the libraries.

We would recommend that your institution evaluate its current orientation efforts. If necessary, appoint a task force to develop and monitor a strong orientation program. Be sure to include clear expectations and link the orientation with other initiatives the campus is engaged in to improve retention.

THE FRESHMAN YEAR

One factor that is becoming increasingly common in the retention literature is the impact the freshman year has on student persistence. Schools that have found success in decreasing high dropout rates generally have targeted special attention to their freshmen class.

Students entering college for the first time bring with them various types of baggage including misconceptions about study time, class requirements and how to fit into the campus environment. Many are away from familiar surroundings for the first time and have to overcome bouts of being homesick. The mechanics of schooling become much more difficult under these circumstances and students often find themselves spending more time dealing with depression than concentrating on mid-terms.

Recognizing these concerns, pro-active institutions are now beginning to provide structured approaches to address these issues. The result on some campuses is an easier adjustment to the college environment.

As mentioned earlier the University of South Carolina is a prime example. They offer a year long freshmen orientation which provides a solid orientation to the university's regulations and resources. Students obtain credit, are made to feel part of a community and through the seminar format are taught things about the campus that will enable them to take advantage of its many resources.

Notre Dame which traditionally has a low attrition rate has a Dean of Freshmen position whose responsibility is to coordinate and monitor services in their Freshmen Year of Studies program, (FYS). The FYS has its own curriculum, support staff, supportive services and sponsors a number of special projects such as field trips and dances to help students feel socially accepted.

While the seminar approached used by the University of South Carolina or the FYS program offered at Notre Dame are preferred programs, funding prohibits some campuses from offering such a comprehensive approach.

Still through creative emphasis, campuses can reassign staff time in ways that allow freshmen to receive extra attention. This is especially significant in large impersonal universities where freshmen classes may number several hundred students.

One innovative approach for those campuses unable to offer a course is to use block registration that enables groups of freshmen to be placed in the same sections. This not only aids in helping them form study blocks but also helps to prevent minority students from being isolated in the classroom.

This can also be accomplished by restricting certain sections or granting priority registration as the need arises.

It also needs to be emphasized here that course selection plays a pivotal role in the freshmen year. This requires quality academic advising. Student's capabilities must be matched in such a way that they can meet the demands of a particular class. Advisors must have a broad knowledge base about course content. They must be familiar with prerequisite requirements and proper sequencing of courses in a particular major.

The dropout ledger is filled with names of freshmen who enrolled in improper courses because it looked good in the catalog. Colleges can ill-afford a sink or swim attitude regarding their freshmen class. Perhaps just the reverse is required. Additional tutoring, advising and faculty attention may be necessary. Noel (1985) claims the first six weeks on campus are critical to students impression of the institution. He implies that universities should use this period to provide transitional activities that will enable students to feel apart of a community.

Other Educators urge a close monitoring of freshmen progress beginning with the fourth week of class. They suggest that an early warning system be adopted where by faculty members would fill out a form *(similar to the one on page 78)* and send it to the student's academic advisor at the first sign of academic difficulty. It would seem that this type of intervention could prove to be an effective strategy in reducing attrition.

It's important to also recognize the student's responsibility during his/her first year on campus. They can't expect to spend excessive amounts of time on social and nonacademic activities and still hope to be academically successful. They need to be told that college is different from high school. There is more freedom and greater self-discipline is required. Much more studying is required, more reading and more homework. It's up to them to set their priorities straight.

The journey they are about to embark on has not been made by most minorities. The opportunity they have been given represents an intellectual smorgasboard of sorts. They have a chance to sample some of the best thinking throughout the ages. Since great things are provided them, great things are expected of them.

The freshmen year can be a wonderful experience. Students don't have to declare a major and they can take courses in various fields to ascertain their interests. When the freshmen year is planned appropriately, it serves as the foundation for one's educational career.

On most predominately white campuses the freshman minority class is not that large to begin with. So the size of the class should easily foster the types of activities that will enable students to feel apart of the institution.

One such activity that has met with much success by colleges is sponsoring a minority student leadership workshop for new minority freshmen. This workshop gives students the skills needed to conduct meetings, plan programs and seek leadership positions on campus. Students are made to feel that they are needed and their contributions are welcomed.

The reason why so much emphasis needs to be placed

on the freshman year is because when minority students make it past that year, the research indicates their retention rates become comparible to that of their white counterparts.

Campuses looking for a place to start tackling high attrition problems would do well to begin with the freshman year.

ACADEMIC ADVISING

It's not unusual to find a first semester freshman's schedule that includes a calculus, chemistry, foreign language, accounting and history course. This selection is fine for some students although it may be less than ideal for others to begin their college experience with. A close look at these courses reveals one thing in common-homework almost every night and tons of reading.

The course selection also assumes a strong background and prior knowledge in rather technical areas. This is a demanding program for any student. Marginal students may find it to be the kiss of death.

Without proper advising, ill informed students often sign up for such classes based on the catalog description. They find themselves in academic difficulty before the semester barely gets underway.

Ideally any student would be able to take a demanding course load and do well. Unfortunately we live in the real world where some student's schools prepare them better than other student's schools. As a result some students need a "catching up" period before they tackle the rigors of such a demanding schedule.

That's where good advising comes in. Good advising let's students know that it's not their intelligence that's being questioned, but their preparation. The schedule that is recommended is based on the skills they brought with them. As their skills improve their course selection will tend to be more challenging. This is done so that students are given the maximum chance to succeed.

In order for students to receive this type of quality advising the advisor must be extremely knowledgeable and competent. The advisor must know what prerequisites are required for certain courses. They need to know what courses can be substituted for other courses. They must possess a substantive knowledge of the curriculum. Successful advisors have more content information on courses than what's provided in the catalog. They contact professors for syallabi, reading lists and course descriptions so they can stay on top of course requirements. Knowledgeable advisors serve on advising and curriculum committees and regularly receive information from such bodies. When they sit down with a student, they have copies of the student's transcripts, test scores and other data that will help provide the best advice possible.

Good advising is usually reflected in the courses students sign up for. By obtaining copies of transcripts its fairly easy to determine whether students are using the advice they've been given. Such monitoring can be used successfully with freshmen students. Coupled with a follow up procedure more serious scheduling problems can be nipped in the bud early on.

It's also helpful if the advisor establishes a personal relationship with the student. Some advisors routinely write the parents of all new freshmen minority students. They explain their role on campus and try to reassure the parents in a friendly personal manner that their sibling is in good hands.

Others let students know that they'll be their contact for the next two years or longer, guaranteeing students consistency in the information they receive.

Effective advising services are not performed in isolation. Advisors must meet regularly to work out problems of freshmen scheduling. They constantly strive to use scheduling and cluster techniques to improve "inclass" retention.

COUNSELING, CAREER/PLACEMENT

Counseling

Who can I turn to...doesn't have to be the theme song for minority students longing for someone to talk to about personal problems. Unfortunately on many campuses the counseling services in place go unused by minority students allowing centers by default to remain unresponsive to minority student needs. Minority students face a unique set of problems at predominately white institutions. (See Chapter 4 for a discussion of these problems.) There are times when these problems become over bearing and students simply need someone to listen.

During this counseling moment it's important that the counseling center have trained counselors capable of providing sensitive guidance to culturally different students.

This is a serious concern because it is the training that counselors receive that allows them to address student's needs. When the training permits a counselor to treat all students the same ignoring cultural signals then the counselor is not in a position to be of much assistance. Students take their problems elsewhere and normally sensitive and caring counselors are left wondering why minority students don't come into the center more often.

An effective counseling program has proven decisive in combating alienation and helping students adjust to college. Sensitive university personnel can help students feel good about being who they are.

The late Johnnie Ruth Clarke who was on the staff at Tallahassee Community College in Tallahassee, Florida felt an effectual retention plan should include the following:

- recruiting outcomes that would attract both sexes to all programs.

- better knowledge of ways to lessen cultural conflict.

- humanistic, sensitive counseling and career guidance.

- peer support within and among minority group members.

- role models on the counseling staff and faculty and in the administrative ranks.

- access to developmental studies to close educational gaps and promote positive personal growth.

- access to placement services that supports self worth and promotes personal economic sufficiency, (Dunston, et al, 1983).

She implies that campus counselors may need to be retrained. They need to know how to select, administer and evaluate assessment instruments. They need an awareness of activities which promote the development of positive self concepts. Counselors should have an understanding of minority students problems from their perspective and then address these problems from both a counseling and instructional perspective.

In looking at black students' counselor preference, Thompson found *"the likelihood of going to the counseling center increased as counselor preference increased,"* (Thompson, 1978). He found that black students preferred black counselors for both personal and educational-vocational problems. He also found that student and counselor sex had no affect on counseling center use.

This is not to suggest that only blacks should counsel blacks but it does imply that non-blacks must be sensitive to cultural factors to be effective in counseling blacks and other minorities. Counseling involves an intimacy of sorts. It involves trust, empathy and a non-judgemental helping attitude.

When a black student sits down with a white counselor to discuss perceived racism on campus, this student wants to know if the counselor can be trusted and if his/her problem will be taken seriously. If not handled properly the situation can be very intimidating and deteriorate very rapidly.

When handled appropriately the counseling center will have gained a supporter and through the word of mouth grapevine would have increased its effectiveness on campus.

While the above scenario may be typical in the sense that counselors wait for students to come in with their problems, some campuses are experimenting with outreach or action counseling. This has proven to be a very good strategy in heading off more serious counseling problems, especially with new freshmen.

Freshmen are asked to fill out an assessment questionnaire during the matriculation period. The questionnaire asks information about their academic backgrounds, interpersonal concerns, personal traits and similar areas. The questionnaire provides a helpful insight into the student's background. The counselor reviews this information and makes contact with the student in a non-threatening manner. Rather than limit the session to a discussion of problems, the counselor shares information about various deadlines, talks about available support services and uses the session as a get acquainted opportunity. Often this initial session is done with a group of freshmen students, helping them to understand the commonality of their concerns.

These types of activities by the counseling center tend to increase minority student use of center services and enhances rapport between students and counselors.

Career/Placement

For many students the only contact they make with the placement office is when graduation is approaching. Placement services have expanded on most campuses during the past decade. Services now range from computerized job listings to allowing students to videotape mock interviews. Resume writing workshops, tips in job hunting, part-time employment opportunities and self improvement seminars are provided on most campuses.

Students undecided about career opportunities can explore with a counselor different types of careers. They can get information that tells them what type of a job a particular major might lead to or what type of additional training they would need to enter the professions.

The placement office is more than just an introduction to the world of work; it's charge is to assist students in the successful culmination of an educational investment by helping them secure employment and educational opportunities commensurate with their preparation and experience. For the most part placement offices are utilized by minority students, especially seniors and graduate students. Outreach efforts need to be targeted at undergraduates to increase their participation. Universities need to do a better job of keeping statistics on the number of minority students served and placed also. There also needs to be stronger linkages between the placement office and workstudy/student employment opportunities on campus. Closer ties between these areas could result in giving students the kind of exposure to careers that is lacking at many institutions.

One of the factors Astin (1975) identified that played a significant part in student's dropping out was indecision about major/career goals. Some universities now offer career planning courses to assist students in their decision making.

In summary, career counseling can influence student persistence in a positive manner.

Learning Resource Center

The literature is clear in identifying academic under-preparedness as a major factor explaining student dropout. As long as American elementary and secondary schools fail to academically prepare them, the poor and racial minority population will continue to enter, college at a disadvantage. When underprepared students enter there has to be remedial type programs available to give them a reasonable chance of succeeding. If this is to be done their academic problems must be diagnosed early on preferably during the matriculation period.

After high risk students' needs have been diagnosed appropriate services must be prescribed.

A model program may be the Early Warning System in place at California State University, Northridge. *Instructors are asked to fill out a form similar to the one previously mentioned on page 78.* This form is returned to the office of origin and appropriate follow up begins.

The real benefit of such a system is that it involves the faculty directly in retention activities. When handled appropriately the message that comes through to students is that faculty and staff care about them.

Although teaching basic skills is still a controversial issue in higher education, recent successes, Noel and Levitz, (1985), have to impress even the staunchest critics.

Remedial education is working primarily because it assumes that underprepared students are not dumb, they simply lack certain academic skills. If they can be taught these skills in a non-stigmatized environment, the research indicates they can compete with their fellow classmates and go on to complete their degrees.

Remedial services have been traditionally rendered either using the classroom approach or tutorial approach. The classroom approach normally involves an instructor teaching a group of under-prepared students reading, writing and mathematical skills. Sometimes the course is offered for credit.

The tutoral approach involves a personal tutor usually skilled in a particular subject area assisting an underprepared student master that subject or skill. The tutorial approach requires trained tutors and adequate space. Many facilities offer a lab like setting and because of the new computer technology, self, tutoring is also available.

The instructional approach requires competent teachers who have high expectations. Some universities are toying with the idea of hiring elementary teachers part-time to teach skill building because of their expertise.

Regardless of which skill building approach is used, it's evident from the literature that supportive services similiar to the Learning Resource Center will help increase retention and graduation rates.

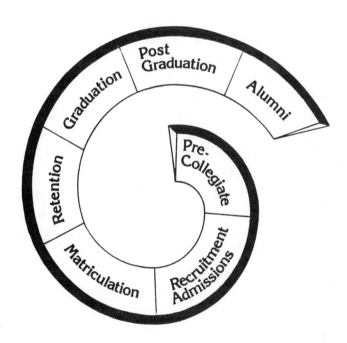

FACULTY INVOLVEMENT

No improvement can be expected in decreasing the attrition rate without faculty leadership and involvement. Collectively and individually faculty have more power to improve retention on campuses that any other group. These are powerful statements yet the role that most faculty play in retention efforts is secondary.

Beal and Noel (1980) found that only 18% of 944 institutions they surveyed involved the faculty in any meaningful manner. This can be explained in part by faculty resistence. Retention is often viewed, at best, as an extra curricular activity; or as someone else's responsibility.

Consider the position that faculty are in. They know which students are repeatedly late for class, unprepared, take few notes, sit at the back of the class, etc. What are they to do with this information. Unfortunately, too many do nothing.

Campuses face a real challenge in getting faculty to understand that assisting in retention doesn't involve a lowering of standards. The literature suggests just the opposite. When the learning environment is improved for some students, it's improved for all.

The retention issue impacts faculty directly. Half empty classrooms mean fewer dollars for instruction, research and the like. Such a situation forces faculty to either jump ship or rethink what their role should be.

It's better for the health of the institution for faculty to put in place preventive measures early on than to find themselves faced with long-term declining enrollments. How important are "standards" under those circumstances?

Let's set aside the self-interest argument and concentrate on a more positive approach to justify faculty involvement with retention. Almost every major study involving retention mentions caring and sensitive faculty as one of the key ingredients for student persistence. Astin (1977) concluded that student-faculty interaction was the most important factor in assessing student satisfaction with their campus. Pantages and

Creedon (1978) reached similar conclusions. Beal and Noel (1980) found the retention factor cited as most important by both two year and four year institutions was the *"caring attitude of faculty and staff"*. When faculty transmit signals that tell students they care the results are usually better motivation, class attendance and involvement in class discussions on the part of students.

Faculty wield tremendous influence over students. Many majors get selected because students admired faculty in a particular department. There are few residence halls or student centers one can enter and not hear discussions about professors.

Students tend to hold professors in high esteem, almost in awe. As a result they have a right to expect fairness. They have a right to expect that the classroom is free of racism and sexism and that information is shared in a way that doesn't belittle them or their culture.

Minority students attending predominately white campuses especially need reassurance upfront from faculty. There is ample research to suggest that minority students educational experiences are qualitatively different than their white counterparts.

If a composite was drawn of the American professor the portrait that would emerge would be that of a middle aged white male with limited experience in interacting with minority students.

This professor's life experiences and educational preparation traditionally place him at odds with students of color. When minority students enter his classroom, more than likely they are the ones who are expected to change.

Nettles' (1982) research concludes that the majority of faculty members at predominately white schools have made no special adjustments in terms of their time allocation, manner of teaching, or curriculum, and most admit that they interact less with their black students than with their white students.

Clearly a shift in faculty attitudes and practices is suggested by Nettles' findings. Without faculty change it is easy to picture minority students being placed in classrooms under less than ideal circumstances. Such an environment contributes to poor class performance and the whole cycle of lower expectancy.

The picture painted above does not have to be overly pessimistic. Faculty can be trained to be effective advisors, mentors and counselors of minority students. Curriculums can be pluralized thereby enhancing the total educational surroundings for all students. Caring faculty recognize the new challenges that minority students represent. They also acknowledge the many positives that minority students bring to the campus as well. They expect minority students to succeed and students respond accordingly. Caring faculty understand that their involvement with students must extend outside the classroom as well. Colleges that have been successful in cutting attrition rates find ways to involve their faculty outside the classroom. This doesn't mean that faculty are expected to attend every minority student function or spend enormous amounts of time engaged in student activities.

The time faculty spend with students has to be a judgement call based on one's schedule, lifestyle and free time available. The point that needs to be made is that quality time spent does make a difference.

Campuses should consider offering incentives to faculty. If the faculty role is as vital as the research indicates then institutional rewards should reflect this importance. Reduced class loads, merit pay increases and similar motivators tell faculty their participation in retention efforts is not only acknowledged but is taken seriously.

This could lead to faculty giving the retention problem the priority it deserves, for example, creating a permanent standing faculty committee on minority student recruitment and retention. This committee could monitor the faculty's significant advisory power over resource allocation, admission decisions, curriculum reform, graduation requirements, special services, grants solicitation, and similar areas.

Many of the programs needed by minority students require faculty support; the limited time faculty have available added to the pressures of publishing and research implies the support needed carries a high premium.

None the less ways must be found to generate faculty advocacy because the record is clear; faculty play a critical role in motivating students to graduate.

Faculty Early Warning System (sample)

Student Monitoring Form *

Student Name/I.D. Number:_____

Course/Section:_____

Instructor:_____

Date Sent:_____

Please rate this student by using the following scale:

excellent	good	fair	poor	very poor	unable to answer
1	2	3	4	5	6

_____ 1. Participates in class discussion

_____ 2. Attendance

_____ 3. Submits class assignments on time

_____ 4. Quality of homework assignments submitted

_____ 5. Quiz results

_____ 6. Test results

_____ 7. Asks for assistance if having difficulty

What grade would you assign the student at this time?

A A/B B B/C C D F OTHER_____

Comments: (where applicable, speak to students' interest shown in class, and any follow up you would recommend).

* This form is to be completed by the Course Instructor/Professor prior to the sixth week of class for those students facing academic difficulty. This form is to be returned to the student's academic advisor.

Student Incentives

When properly motivated students make superb recruiters, peer counselors, tutors and helpers who can tremendously enhance a university's overall retention efforts. The enthusiasm and idealism they bring to projects is heartening and when this energy is channeled into a positive force the results can be astounding.

When one thinks of the many fine presentations, seminars, talent shows, etc., that students have created, planned and implemented then one begins to appreciate the marvelous talent and knowledge they bring to our campuses.

Too much attention is given to student's weaknesses rather than their strengths; strengths that often go unmeasured by standardized tests. These strengths need to be nurtured and supported. Many minority students have a deep social conscience and are interested in "giving back" to the community. Developmental workshops stressing leadership and organizational training can give students the type of skills that encourage their involvement in campus activities. Opportunities like these help to motivate students and allows them to feel needed on campus. When campuses create the right atmosphere it seems that minority student interaction falls in place.

A supportive environment is one in which student growth is expected and fostered. Student organizations are promoted and given the resources necessary to function.

When there is advocacy for minority students on a campus the results are students helping to bring in new students; and students helping each other make it through.

INNOVATIVE RETENTION PROGRAMS

(These samples were taken from press releases and student newspapers.)

Orientation Programs

Minority Student Unity Reception
The Asian-American Coalition holds an Annual Minority Unity Reception at Cornell to bring a closer unity among the various minority groups on campus.

Get Acquainted Day
The Office of Minority Affairs at Central Michigan University sponsor a Get Acquainted Day designed to give minority students a chance to get acquainted with one another and with CMU faculty members. Get Acquainted Day activities include free food, jazz and short speeches by college officials and minority student leaders.

Entire Campus Involved in Diversity Program
Colby College in Northern Maine launched a year long, campus wide study program called "Celebrating Diversity and Confronting Intolerance." Nationally known speakers visited the campus throughout the year to lecture and participate in discussions on minority issues. The entire college was asked to participate in this voluntary project. Almost every ethnic minority was discussed during the year.

Group Forms to Improve Communication
An interracial organization called the Minority/Majority Concerns Committee at Michigan State University was formed to open lines of communication between blacks and whites.

All Campus Minority Reception
The Graduate School and the WSA Minority Affairs Committee holds an "All Campus Minority Reception" for the University of Wisconsin-Madison minority students and faculty. Attendees meet with students, faculty, staff, state and community representatives.

The Freshman Year

Indian Honor Society

Northern Arizona University's Dr. Frank Dukepoo founded the American Indian Honor Society as a way to encourage Indians to be successful academically and to combat some of the negative stereotypes held by non-Indians. Members provide assistance to incoming freshmen and to activities of other Indian student organizations on campus, participate in high school tutorial programs; hold annual Honor Banquets and have provided financial assistance for such projects as Students of the Month Awards and participation in the Navajo Tribal Parade and Fair.

Mentor Program Experiences Success

The University of Texas's mentor program has experienced positive results. Coordinated out of the Dean of Student's Office the program matches faculty members with minority students in an effort to increase minority students retention. Faculty serve as role models, provide students with someone to confide in and motivate students to achieve academically.

Academic Advising

New Re-Entry Admissions Program Gives Adults Second Chance At A University Education

San Francisco State University now has a special admissions procedure for adults wishing to start or complete a university education. The program is specifically designed for individuals who would not qualify for regular admission into the university. The new Re-Entry Admission Program (R.A.P.) is open to individuals 25 years old or above who have not been enrolled as a full-time student for more than one academic term within the previous five years. Prospective students are interviewed by an academic counselor to assess their educational goals.

Counseling/Career Development

Peer Counseling

At Kutztown University, through its Peer Counseling Program the university provides student to student counseling in such areas as academic advising and personal concerns. Peer counselors are selected on the basis of their earned grade point average, leadership qualities and ability to relate to others.

Learning Resource Center

OSU Study Group Program Prevents Drop Outs

The office of Black Students Programs at Ohio State University (OSU) has a program to prevent minority students from dropping out. Study groups in target courses, (i.e., beginning math and English classes), have from three to ten students. The students arrange their own session time and study methods. Upperclassmen and graduate students conduct the sessions themselves. The program also has tutors available to assist. If the program proves to be successful, the office wants to include psychology and biology classes for the spring quarter. The office would eventually like to see the program include every course and make it available to graduate students as well.

Proper Way to Use Standardized Tests

Milwaukee, Wis.--Marquette University's Educational Opportunity program offered training to over 100 counselors and instructors from the midwest on appropriate uses of standardized tests and other instruments in evaluating "disadvantaged" students.

Faculty Involvement

Faculty Student Interaction Encouraged

Michael Gordon, Dean of Students at University of Indiana-Bloomington, writing a guest column in the student newspaper, encourages greater interaction between students and faculty. Mr. Gordon said he recieved a "flood of positive responses" to a questionnaire he sent faculty members requesting the extent of their desire to be involved in student life. Citing several ways in which faculty could put this desire into action, ranging from residence hall programs to inviting students home, Dean Gordon introduced a new program run by the Student Advocate Corps (SAC). SAC consists of retired professors who staff the Student Advocate's office. The professors help students resolve problems by listening, making referrals and giving advice.

International Curriculum

Hope College received an award from the Exxon Education Foundation to support a faculty development program designed to integrate an international perspective throughout the College's curriculum. The goal of the program is to provide every Hope College Student with a "mature, thoughtful exposure to an international perspective in a number of different academic courses". Campus administrators feel that the traditional Western-European approach to curricula matters is to a great extent outmoded. This new approach will allow Hope to explore ways in which this can be developed, such as, incorporating literature from the Third World into modern language courses, providing for cross cultural analysis of the family in sociology courses and other such methods.

Minority Visitors Program

Indiana University-Bloomington announced the creation of a program to attract Blacks with special one-year faculty appointments. The Minority Visitors program began in the

fall of the 82-83 academic year. A special fund was set aside by
the campus administration to help pay for the program.

Student Incentives

Project Grasp

Project Grasp's (sponsored by the Texas Association
of Mexican American Medical Students) main objective is
directed at attracting more Minorities into the medical professions. The project focuses its efforts on "matching" potential
students (at one of the eight medical schools in Texas) with
successful medical students on a one-to-one basis in order to
provide the support and contacts needed to enter medical
school.

Academic Incentives

The Black Student Union at the Univ. of Kentucky-
Lexington stressed academics by implementing an incentive
plan that provided cash awards to students who excelled
academically. There were 4 categories of awards that students
could have received payment for: Greek, freshmen, upper class
students and most improved. This incentive was planned to
help reduce the dropout rate of black students.

La Hora De Espanol

"La Hora De Espanol"-The Organization of Latin
American Students at Northern Illinois University (NIU)
developed a program to help students experiencing difficulty in
Spanish class as well as providing an outlet for Latinos who
just want to rap. Interested students attend a weekly la hora de
espanol (the Spanish hour) and participate in activities completely in Spanish. Students can concentrate on improving their
vocabulary and grammar skills as well as learn word games
like scrabble in Spanish.

Positive Images Through Radio
    Fisk University students use radio as an avenue to provide the people of Nashville with a black musical perspective and seek to balance the negative images of black people presented in the media through music, poetry, and creative public affairs programming.

Black Student Newspaper
    Black students at the University of Oklahoma published a student newspaper, *Unity* to provide broader coverage of Black student affairs. Black journalism students write most of the articles and the paper is published twice a semester.

Black Student Alliance
    Black Students in Kentucky formed the First Kentucky Alliance of Black Student organizations and hosted a leadership conference to strengthen the efforts of Kentucky Blacks in Higher Education in the 80's.

Third World Desk
    The University of California Student Lobby in Sacramento instituted a Third World Desk to serve as a resource for Minority aids and access to the administration at both the local and system wide levels and to the legislature. The desk idea has proved effective in getting Minority Students involved.

Hotline Installed for Minority Students
    Minority students at the University of Texas have their own hotline. The Committee on Minority Affairs created MACline to answer questions of minority students and provide information which concerns them. MACline operates in the Graduate School of Business. It has two phone lines-each offering a separate service. One line is answered 6-10 p.m. by volunteer students who answer questions about financial aid, University facilities, Learning Skills Center, etc. The other line plays a tape with information about campus activities for

---

minority students. Students can inquire about the Black
greek system or social events for international students. Members of the MACline sub-committee contacted over 40 Minority Organizations on campus to explain MACline and solicit
data for the prerecorded message of campus activities. They
also use volunteers from these organizations to answer the
phone line.

Black Unity

To promote togetherness and cooperation between
Black males and females in Divison III colleges, students for
Black Development at Central College in Pella, Iowa sponsor
an annual co-ed basketball tournament and soul food dinner.

UA Appoints Retention Director

The Office of Minority Student Affairs at the University
of Arizona (UA) created and appointed an associate director
for retention. The retention program is designed to assist
students with collegiate problems and provide firsthand
experience with various cultures.

News Stories Help Retention

Positive news stories about black students distributed
by the Information Services office was partially attributed to
increasing the black student enrollment at the University of
Florida-Gainsville.

Multicultural Materials Fair

The School of Education at Kansas University sponsored a multicultural fair to acquaint students and staff with
material that can be used to provide a multicultural education.
The fair included exhibits, films and ethnic music.

Retention Resources

Nationalities Service Center
1300 Spruce St.
Philadelphia, PA 19107   215/893-8400

Guide to Resource Organizations for Minority Language
Groups available from the National Clearinghouse for Bilingual Education InterAmerican Research Association Inc.
1555 Wilson Blvd, Suite 605
Rosslym,VA 22209

United States Student Association
1012 14th St., NW Ste. 207
Washington, DC 20005   202/347-8772

National Council of Educational Opportunity Associations
1025 Vermont Ave., NW, Suite 310
Washington, DC 20005   202/347-7430

National Association for Campus Activities (NACA)
P.O. Box 6828
Columbia, SC 29260   803/782-7121

TEN INEXPENSIVE STRATEGIES TO RECRUIT AND RETAIN MINORITY STUDENTS

1. Personalized letter sent to parents of freshman students

Surveys conducted by the author confirm that freshmen are still greatly influenced by their parents. A personal, friendly letter of introduction allows you to establish contact with a student's parent(s), and possibly channel some of that influence to increase their son's and daughter's involvement on campus.

2. Positive press releases mailed to hometown papers

There are few things as motivating as good publicity. One positive story in his/her hometown paper (sent out by the Public Affairs Office) has proven effective and the author is aware of at least one campus that partially credits such publicity as helping to increase retention rates. Once the publicity hits home, and students have been congratulated by hometown friends, they tend to strive even harder on campus.

3. Regular articles in student newspaper

We created two stacks of student newspapers (when looking through them for information for this book). One stack had articles (other than sports or crime) about minorities and the other stack did not.

The stack that did not have any articles was about five times the size of the one that did. After looking at hundreds of such publications, you begin to wonder why minorities are missing from the press. If any publication should reflect diversity it's the campus newspaper at an institution of higher learning. When students see themselves, their friends and their culture given coverage in a variety of settings, they tend to feel a part of the campus.

4. Involving Minority Student Organizations

Student Organizations represent experience, talent and bundles of energy. When properly channeled they can help the university in recruiting and retaining students. Campuses that provide student organizations with leadership and similar developmental training find the investment pays off.

5. Create a Minority student Advisory Council

When there are few student organizations and little participation in student government, residence halls, etc., an advisory council can fill the void. A representative council can help increase student interaction and participation.

6. Encourage a Student "Replacement" campaign

Minority student organizations can be encouraged to sponsor a campaign in which (so inclined) graduating seniors and those deciding not to come back attempt to replace themselves with another student. Successful students can be honored at end of year student sponsored banquets. Student organizations have to assume the leadership role for this strategy to effectively work.

7. Have faculty create a permanent retention committee

A standing committee ensures the issues are receiving the attention they deserve while involving faculty directly in the process.

8. Sponsor get acquainted meetings by sex

Friendships contribute to a feeling of belonging. Black faculty and staff on the Newark campus-Rutgers University devised a program for black males to get together. A directory of black students by class and major was compiled and used by students to form study groups. Social activities, mentor relationships, and new friendships were the outcome. A similar group was formed for women. Now both groups are actively involved in retention efforts.

9. Create a "town-gown" committee

Students may avoid some colleges because of the reputation of the town. Institutions located in small or rural communities face even greater challenges. A town-gown committee can help smooth the transition that students must make.

10. Involve minority alumni

Create a Minority Alumni organization. Such organizations raise funds, sponsor annual workshops/conferences, and help recruit and retain faculty as well as students.

GRADUATION ISSUES
_____

   With so much emphasis placed on recruitment and
retention it's important not to lose sight of the purpose of all
these efforts-graduation.
   The intent must be to recruit with the goal of graduating minority students. Although nationally there has been
some decline in students selection of majors in humanities and
education, a substantial number of minority students still
major in such fields.
   Young tries to explain this in part by arguing that
white culture emphasizes intellectualism and the scientific
disciplines, while Blacks and other minorities are predisposed
toward the humanities. He says in order to reverse this trend
colleges must focus on:

   1) selecting Black students who can adjust to the college's social
   system, 2) developing goal oriented behaviors among Blacks that stress
   scientific and intellectual pursuits 3) emphasizing that Black and dominant
   value systems can coexist and 4) providing social and psychological support
   for Black students, (Young, 1983).

   Although Dr. Young's recommendations are important,
his first one runs the risk of being misinterpreted and could
be used by colleges to justify recruiting only middle class
minority students.
   There is little disagreement among educators that we
have a shortage of minorities in just about every field. Perhaps
a goal worth pursuing nationally is to work for parity in degree
production. If this is to occur (just for Black students only) it
has been estimated something like 100,000 baccalaureates
would need to be produced annually. We are currently operating at about 60,000 annually. To achieve parity in the professions and for Ph.D.'s would require about 3,000 degree recipients, far more than the thousand or less currently being
earned by Blacks. Table 22 provides more detailed information on the types and numbers of degrees earned.
   Still another problem faced by minority students is the

length of time it takes to graduate. Goodrich (1977) estimated that only 5 out of 30 Black students who enter a four year college graduate on schedule. In a similar study Gosman (1982) found that minority students take longer than whites to graduate. This effects students in terms of heavier financial aid debts.

Administrators may need to investigate the value of academic and career counseling that is being made available to minority students. The investigation should uncover what areas minority students are majoring in and analyze whether students are receiving the needed guidance to explore other majors.

Additionally, the placement rate of minority students needs to be evaluated. Graduating students who land appropriate jobs tend to serve as role models for undergraduate students.

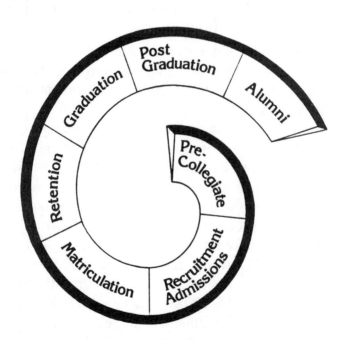

GRADUATION INITIATIVES

- Have academic advising and career placement offices sponsor joint workshops for minority students.

- Encourage students to have a degree summary made annually that lists all the courses they have taken and all the courses they need to take in order to graduate.

- Have various departments sponsor "Consider Us" informational nights for students to answer questions about majors, career opportunties, etc.

- Bring minority role models currently working in a variety of areas on campus for an inspirational rap session with students.

- Encourage minority students groups to recognize students that graduate each year and make graduation recognition type activites a priority in their overall programming efforts.

Table 22

Types & Number of Degrees Earned by race (1980-81)

Year	Degree	Total	White	Black	Hispanic	Asian	Amer. Indian
80-81	Bachelors	912,211	807,319	60,673	21,832	18,794	3,593
80-81	Masters	272,126	241,216	17,133	6,461	6,282	1,034
80-81	Doctors	28,636	25,908	1,265	456	877	130
80-81	First Prof.	70,671	64,551	2,931	1,541	1,456	192

Percentage by race (1980-81)

		White	Black	Hispanic	Asian	Amer. Indian
BA/BS	912,211	88.5	6.6	2.3	2.0	.39
MA/MS	272,126	88.6	6.2	2.3	2.3	.37
Doct.[1]	28,636	90.4	4.4	1.5	3.0	.45
First Prof[2]	70,671	91.3	4.1	2.1	2.0	.27

Source: adapted from U.S. Department of Education, Office for Civil Rights, *Data on Earned Degrees Conferred by Institutions of Higher Education by Race, Ethnicity, and Sex Academic Year 1980-1981*: Tables 109, 109a, 109b, and 110.

1. Includes Ph D., Ed D., and comparable degrees at the Doctorial level.

2. Includes Dentistry (D.D.S or DMD) Medicine (M.D.), Pharmacy, Veterinary Medicine, Chiropractic, Law and Theological degrees.

POST-GRADUATION ISSUES

In most indices of progress, statistics on Black and Hispanic participation in higher education show a serious decline in the last five years.

When looking at the data, the small number of minorities makes comparative analysis almost meaningless. The actual numbers as well as the percentages must be examined in order to get a clearer picture of what's really occuring.

The National Advisory Committee on Black Higher Education and Black Colleges and Universities issued a report a few years back entitled, *"The Status of Blacks in Graduate and Professional Schools"*. The report claimed that Black participation in graduate and professional education remains surprisingly low and in recent years has actually worsened. Since 1977 the number and percentage of Black Ph.D's has steadily declined.

In the physical sciences and engineering fields, non-resident aliens earned 13 times and 41 times as many doctorates, respectively as American born black Americans according to the report.

The proportion of Black and Chicano students has decreased in medical and law school. Historically Black schools continue to produce a disproportionate number of Black master and Ph.D graduates. Nearly 40 percent of all dental degrees conferred come from historically Black institutions.

Financial obstacles appear to be the leading reason for the lack of progress in minority participation in advance study.

The number of minority students receiving fellowship awards are so low that it raises serious doubts concerning a national commitment to resolving this dilemma.

Among 1978 doctorate recipients, Blacks received 2 of 422 National Science Foundation (NSF) traineeship awards, 16 of 725 NSF fellowship awards, 243 of 13,193 institutional teaching assistantships, and 156 of 10,206 institutional research assistantships, (source: The Black Collegian October/ November 1981, p. 87).

Among the 1978 recipients, there were virtually no federal or institutional awards to Blacks in engineering or physical and life sciences. Unfortunately the situation has improved little since 1981.

These figures point to lost opportunities when you consider an increasing number of careers and jobs choices require preparation beyond the baccalaureate degree.

Graduate schools need to do a better job of outreach to minority undergraduate students. The best place to start might be their own undergraduate departments. If the school of social work, for example, has twenty undergraduates in its program, those students should be contacted for possible graduate school and told about opportunities elsewhere.

Statistics from the National Urban League and the U.S. Equal Employment Opportunity Commission find that only about 4.4% of the nation's faculty members are Black. About half of these are at predominantly White institutions. According to a report published in 1982 by the College and University Personnel Association and confirmed by the Digest of Educational Statistics (1988) white males outnumber women and minority faculty by about three to one. So it's still possible for white and third world students to go through their entire undergraduate and graduate experience and never have the opportunity to be taught by a woman or a black professor.

Universities need to expand their efforts to include the recruitment and retention of minority graduate students and faculty. Affirmative action policies might need to be established and enforced concerning TA's, project and research assistants.

We must keep in mind that dollars used to fund graduate employment opportunities for the most part are public monies so we have a right to expect that tax dollars won't be used to perpetuate exclusion and discrimination in post graduate collegiate opportunities.

POST-GRADUATE INITIATIVES

- sponsoring graduate school opportunity nights for minority juniors and seniors.

- having graduate departments send timely news and announce ments to students enrolled in their undergraduate programs keeping them abreast of graduate opportunities.

- providing practicum and internship opportunities for under graduate minority students with the goal of preparing them for TA slots.

- establishing early identification programs to locate students who will succeed in graduate school.

- advertising graduate opportunities in minority oriented publications.

- increasing post-doctoral opportunities for minority staff.

Innovative Post Graduate Programs
(These samples were taken from press releases and campus newspapers)

Affirmative Action Directory
The California Legislature directed the California Postsecondary Education Commission to establish and maintain a registry of names and qualifications of ethnic minorities and women who are available for employment in academic and administrative positions in higher education. The participation of job applicants and of institutions is voluntary. No fee is charged the applicant or the institution for use of the registry. Registry forms and instructions may be obtained by writing to the: REGISTRY, California Postsecondary Education Commission, 1020 12th Street, Sacramento, California 95814.

Oklahoma Regents Awards Doctoral Study Grants
The Oklahoma State Regents for Higher Education awards minority graduate and professional students doctoral awards. The awards for Doctoral Study Grants are given to students who complete 30 credits or more.

Network Designed to Increase MBA Degree for Minorities

The Minority Admissions Recruitment Network
(MARN) is designed to increase the number of minority
students in graduate management programs. Norman
Campbell of Southern Methodist University and Brent
Johnson of Atlanta University Graduate School of Business
pioneered its existence. MARN provides minority students
with a network of colleges and universities so they can explore
the institutions. The organization's aim is to offer a variety of
graduate programs that are not readily available to minority
students; to encourage minority undergraduate students to
pursue their MBA degrees and assist in their retention and
subsequent graduation.

Hispanic Leadership Fellows Program

The Hispanic Leadership Fellows program (sponsored
by the New Jersey Department of Higher Education in cooperation with the Woodrow Wilson National Fellowship Foundation and the American Council of Education) is designed to
identify a select group of Hispanic faculty and administrators
employed by college and Universities in New York, New
Jersey and Pennsylvania. This group of leaders is identified as
having the potential to move into top and middle management positions. Each year 30 fellows are selected to participate in the training program designed to develop skills in
management, communication, budgeting and decision-making
with emphasis on practical applications and cross cultural
dimensions. The program runs the course of the academic year.

American Indian Physicians Create Program

The Association of American Indian Physicians,
headquartered in Oklahoma City has designed a 3 day workshop to help Indian students successfully select, apply and gain
admission to health professions schools.

POST-GRADUATION RESOURCES

Organization of Chinese Americans
2025 Eye St NW Suite 926
Washington, DC 20006   202/223-5500

National Network of Hispanic Women
Center for Research on Women
12021 Wilshire Boulevard
Los Angeles, CA 90025

Association of American Indian Physicians   (A.A.I.P.)
10015 S. Pennsylvania, Bldg. D
Oklahoma City, OK 73139   405/692-1202

Association of Black Psychologists
P.O. Box 2929
Washington, DC 20013

National Association of Black Accountants Inc.
300 I Street, NE
Washington, DC 20002   202/543-6656

National Society of Black Engineers
344 Commerce Street
Alexandria, Va 22314   703/549-2207

The Black Collegians Guide to Graduate Fellowships
for Minority Students
c/o Black Collegian: the National Magazine of Black College
Students
1240 S. Broad St.
New Orleans, LA 70125

ALUMNI ISSUES

When it comes to choosing a college or university the best "mirror" for a prospective student can be the institution's successful alumni. Minority alumni are a valuable asset in the recruitment and retention cycle. Because these former students have made their way through the institution's educational system they serve as proof to other potential minority students that graduation is a possible achievement. Their success after having received an education proves to students the value of higher education. Therefore, it makes sense for post secondary institutions to enlist the help of former students in recruiting potential students. Campuses miss a real opportunity by not involving their minority alumni on a larger scale. Who can better "sell" a university than one of its former students?

At Duke University a Black alumni association was formed to support the university. Even though some of the alumni had reservations toward the university, they were interested in helping their alma mater because they realized their education contributed to their present successes. The association is involved in fund raising, recruitment of minority students, faculty and other areas.

Minority alumni serve campuses by the advice they are able to offer students in adjusting to a new environment. They can relate their own experiences and give students a sense of the history of an institution. An example of this might be the program that was sponsored by the department of Pan African studies at Kent State where two of its alumni were featured speakers on the role of Black studies programs in the 80's. They told students how Kent State had changed over the years and discussed what Black students had achieved and what they must do to achieve new goals. They encouraged student involvement in campus activities.

Although the primary role of the Native American Alumni Association at Dartmouth is to recruit students, the association also acts as a support group for each other.

Because its members are spread out all over the country, they publish a newsletter to keep their members up to date on the happenings of the college, on the individual activities of graduates, and various job opportunities.

Several universities realizing the value of minority alumnus groups have started actively encouraging their formation. One such campus is the University of California, Santa Barbara. According to a press release they had a research project developed in order to find out more about their 1,500 Chicano graduates. At Syracuse University they held a "Coming Back Together" reunion for minority graduates. Pennsylvania State University hosted a two day minority alumni conference. The two day training conference was aimed at supporting the university's minority recruitment and retention efforts.

The extent to which Black and minority groups get involved in alumni activities is often the best gauge of determining whether they feel a part of the campus or not.

The literature that we uncovered addressing this issue suggests that those institutions which provide their students with a sense of tradition and sense of belonging reap greater involvement from former students in fund raising and related alumni affairs.

ALUMNI INITIATIVES

- the creation of a minority alumni advising body.

- the development of alumni traditions that can be passed
  down from one graduating class to the next.

- the pluralization of alumni staff, ensuring the availability of a
  minority staff person to address the needs of minority alumni.

- the development of a multicultural wing in the alumni house
  where portraits, awards, accomplishments, etc., are displayed.

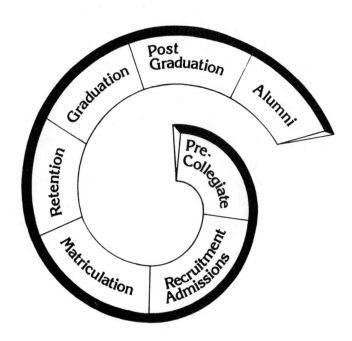

FINANCIAL AID ISSUES

Based on the statistics cited in table 23 and the increasing costs of attending college its logical to conclude that most minority students will need some form of assistance. For a number of reasons, many Minority families are not in a position to pay for college. A recent Census Bureau study based on 1984 financial statistics found that the typical black family had less than a tenth of the assets of a white family. Hispanic families fared on slightly better. Given the present political and economic climate, universities face great challenges in using their financial aid dollars to maintain equal opportunity goals.

This becomes increasingly difficult in light of significant decreases in federal dollars. An actual reduction in federal dollars by 19 per cent occurred between 1980 and 1984, (The College Entrance Examination Board, 1984, p.2). The number of black students attending institutions of higher learning declined during this period as a result.

Looking back in the late sixties to mid 70's when the minority student enrollment experienced a dramatic increase, financial aid played a key role in making that phenomenon possible. This relationship of minority student enrollment patterns and financial aids needs to be strengthened if this country is to get back on the equity track.

Given the cutbacks previously mentioned, a general problem is that many campuses don't have enough money to meet the needs of all eligible students. Traditionally some form of distribution system is implemented which usually results in all students having a portion of their need unmet.

For the poorest students with no resources to fall back on, one abnormal or unforseen expense can block their attendance. Financial aid is clearly an area where differences of treatment can be justified. Treating all students the same would continue to disadvantage low income students.

Policymakers should recognize that equity considerations involve more than sameness; they must acknowledge that some students enter the institutions with greater needs and the

Table 23

MEDIAN INCOME OF HISPANIC, BLACK, AND WHITE FAMILIES: 1972-1982

Year	Median family income (in constant 1982 dollars)			Hispanic family income as percent of white income
	Hispanic	Black	White	
1972	$17,790	$14,922	$25,107	71
1973	17,836	14,877	25,777	69
1974	17,594	14,765	24,110	71
1975	16,140	14,835	24,110	67
1976	16,390	14,766	24,823	66
1977	17,141	14,352	25,124	68
1978	17,518	15,166	25,606	68
1979	18,255	14,590	25,689	71
1980	16,242	13,989	24,176	67
1981	16,401	13,266	23,517	70
1982	16,227	13,598	24,603	66

Source: U.S. Bureau of the Census. "Money Income and Poverty Status of Families and Persons in the United States: 1981" (Advance Data from the March 1982 Current Population Survey), *Current Population Reports,* Series P-60, No. 134, July 1982, Table 3 U.S. Bureau of the Census. "Money Income and Poverty Status of Families and Persons in the United States: 1982," *"Current Population Reports,* Series P-60, No. 140, 1983, Table 2.

Table 23 illustrates the economic position of Hispanics and Blacks relative to Whites. Hispanics as a group fall between Whites and Blacks although Puerto Ricans fare worse than Blacks. More over the position of Hispanics and Blacks has not improved relative to Whites over the past decade. *Hispanics: Challenges and Opportunities,* A working paper from the Ford Foundation P. 23 & 24, 1984.

financial aid policy must address those needs. An initial task
for financial aid administrators is to determine the number and
percentage of students with unmet need. Philosophically it
seems that the poorest students should have their needs met
first. These are the students who simply could not attend
without financial assistance.

Many campuses are using internal funds to supplement
federal dollars as a way of guaranteeing full funding for low
income students. Others spearhead scholarship fundraising
campaigns to make up the difference.

However far too many are requiring low income students to borrow guaranteed student loans or some other loan
to fill their unmet need. What is emerging is such students are
graduating with tremendous loan debts.

Administrators need to establish what a manageable
debt level is. Students need to be informed annually of their
current loan debt and what that debt might be if they continue
their present course of borrowing. They need to be informed
of loan consolidation programs similar to those sponsored by
the Student Loan Marketing Association.

Institutional policy ought to be flexible enough when
high loan debt students have legitimate needs, money is set
aside from unrestricted general funds to provide grants to
sustain reasonable loan debt levels.

Sensitive policies like these are called for if minority
students are not to be handicapped once they graduate from
college. Being saddled with a traditional ten year loan debt in
today's job market is an enormous burden for anyone to bear.

What can campuses do to prevent such a situation
from occurring? A primary consideration must include disseminating information to students. Workshops can be offered
on budgeting, money management and alternative financial aid
sources.

Students need to know they have to apply for financial
aid annually and that they must apply on time to receive full

consideration for grants. Students need to know they may have to fill out several forms when seeking aid; an institutional form, the financial aid form (FAF) which requires a fee and is used to determine a student's eligibiltity for all federal aid and many states offer their own aid programs which call for a separate application.

Students need to know the options they have - that is, whether a loan can be substituted for employment or a scholarship etc. A financial aids package normally includes grants, scholarships, loans, and some form of workstudy/student employment. While one's award appears to be cemented in stone, it is to some extent negotiable. Higher than normal medical bills, higher costs for equipment and supplies - based on one's major, marital status, self-help levels and similar categories are justifications for financial-aid adjustments.

The better informed the student body is about financial aid policies the better it will be able to maintain manageable debt levels.

Innovative Financial Aid Programs
(These examples were taken from press releases and student newspapers)

Saturday Workshop for Potential Students
Mills College offered free Saturday workshops for families of college bound students who wanted help understanding and completing financial aid application forms required by the State of California for college financial aid.

To Blunt The Sting Of Federal Cuts
The U. of Tennessee-Chattanooga expanded its financial aid program to include guarantee loans for honor students and off-campus jobs for others. The two additions to the financial aid program will help as many as 700 students, many of whom lost aid under Reagan administration budget cuts. By intensifying the search for off-campus, part-time work UTC officials hope to guarantee students jobs before they enroll.

Loans for Students

A. *In-house loan programs*- many schools are considering the development or expansion of in-house loan programs available to students from their private endowment.

B. *Parent loan programs*-some schools are working with lending institutions to make loans available at low interest rates to parents of undergraduates.

C. *Corporate repayment loans*-some schools are trying to involve corporations in the repayment of their employees' student loans as tax deductible gifts.

D. Colleges are developing a number of different programs to help ease the burden of rising tuition costs. Extended payment plans, in which payments for a year's tuition can be made on a monthly basis, extended over the full calendar year or even beyond graduation are being considered.

Northland College Updates 'Earn While You Learn' Theory

Northland recently guaranteed its 500-plus students $500 to $1,500 a year in on-campus employment to supplement other financial aid. Officials want to increase the work fund by $100,000 a year for the next three years to help reverse the school's five-year enrollment decline.

FINANCIAL AID RESOURCES

Financial Aid Directories

The Directory of Financial Aids for Minorities, 1989-1990 Gail Ann Schlacter. TGC/Reference Service Press, 1100 Industrial Road, Suite #9, San Carlos, CA 94070.

While numerous sources offer information on financial aids programs open to all segments of society, rarely do these cover more than a few of the programs designed primarily or exclusively for minority groups. As a result, many advisors, counselors, librarians, scholars, researchers, and students remain uninformed about the impressive array of financial aids programs established for minorities. In today's political and economic climates, the minority student and researcher, more than ever, need access to resources to finance continuing education or training. *The Directory of Financial Aids for Minorities*, 1989-1990 provides comprehensive, up-to-date information about the special resources set aside for Asians, Blacks, Hispanics, Native Americans (American Indians, Hawaiians, Eskimos, Samoans), and minority groups in general. The programs described are sponsored by government agencies, professional organizations, corporations, sororities, fraternities, foundations, religious groups, educational associations and military/veterans organizations.

Directory of Special Programs and Financial Assistance for Black and Other Minority Group Students. Urban League of Westchester, 61 Mitchell Place, White Plains, NY 10601, 914/ 428-6300.

Scholarships, Fellowships and Loans Volume VII. Available for $75 from Bellman Publishing, P.O. Box 164, Arlington, MA 02174.

Student Work, Study, Travel Catalog. Available from the Council on International Educational Exchange, 205 E. 42nd St., Ny, NY 10017.

Financial Aid

A Selected list of Post-Secondary Education Opportunities for Minorities and Women. U.S. Dept. of Health, Education, Welfare, Office of Bureau of Higher Education, Room 4913, ROB-3, 400 Maryland Avenue, S.W., Washington, D.C. 20202.

The Department of Education has released a report on methods of securing financial aid. For information contact: Student Liaison, Department of Education, FOB MS 6350, Rm 3073, 400 Maryland Avenue SW, Washington, DC 20202.

Education Fellowships for Indian Students. Office of Indian Education has grants for Indian students interested in courses in business administration, natural resources, medicine, engineering, law, education and related fields. Grants range from $2,300-$14,000. The average grant received is $5,000. For application or information, contact: Office of Indian Education, Department of Education, 400 Maryland Ave. S.W., Washington, DC 20202.

You may also refer to the following resources available from the addresses below.

Educational Financial Aids: A Guide to Selected Fellowships, Scholarships and Internships in Higher Education, American Association of University Women, Sales Office, 2401 Virginia Avenue, NW, Washington, DC 20037, 202/785-7700. $4/copy.

Aid: A Partial List of Resources for Women, 1982 Project on the Status and Education of Women, Association of American Colleges, 1818 R Street, NW, Washington, DC 20009, 202/387-1300. For $2.50 a copy.

The Ambitious Student's Guide to Scholarship and Loans Is available for $2.50 (prepaid) from the Project on the Status of Women, Association of American Colleges, 1818 R Street,

NW, Washington, D.C. 20009. Checks should be made payable to AAC/PSEW. Bulk rates are available.

American College Testing Program, Iowa City, Iowa 52240. Has a withdrawal form that asks the types of questions that will assist administrators in helping students stay in school or at leaste find out the reasons why students leave.

The Directory of Special Programs for Minority Group Members, Garrett Park Press, P.O. Box 190F, Garrett Park, MD 20896. Available in its fourth edition and costs $22.50. The directory includes career information services, employment skills banks and financial aid sources.

Financial Aid Booklets

Garrett Park Press, Garrett Park, MD 20896 has a series of booklets specializing in financial aid programs for Minority students (graduate and undergraduate) in the fields of Allied Health, Business, Education, Engineering, Law, Mass Communications, Medicine, and Science. In addition, each booklet contains an employment outlook summary and a tabulation of Minority group members currently employed in the field. Each booklet costs $3.00.

Five Federal Aid Programs-A Student Consumer's Guide, U.S. Department of Education, Consumer Information Center, Pueblo, CO 81009.

Mortgaged Futures: How to Graduate from School Without Going Broke. Explains how students can apply for financial aid, set up financial plans and seek counseling, provides lists of available programs and resources. Contact: $10.95, postage paid, from Hope Press, P.O. Box 40611, Washington, DC 20016; 202/337-4507.

Scholarships, Fellowships, and Loans News Service and Counselor Information Services. Bellman Publishing Co., P.O. Box 34937, Bethesda, Maryland 20817

Student Aid and the Urban Poor, Ford Foundation, P.O. Box 559, Naugatuck, CT 06770.

The College Board. College Scholarship Service, 888 Seventh Ave., NY, NY 10106. Has publications that describe financial aids to parents.

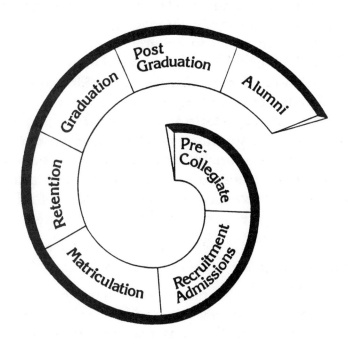

SOCIAL FACTORS IMPACTING RETENTION

Universities are highly complex social systems. The better students are integrated into these systems, the more likely their perseverance and graduation.

A general difficulty faced by minority students is integrating into the system. This difficulty is exacerbated by social factors that stand as barriers prohibiting minority students from enjoying all of the benefits and advantages that universities offer.

Minority students react to these barriers in a number of ways. The high attrition rate nationally testifies to one self damaging way in which students respond. Bressler (1967) suggests that students of color must choose among several social options: assimilation, cultural pluralism or separation. Gibbs (1974) found that Blacks engaged in four models of coping behavior. This she labeled as, withdrawal, separation, assimilation and affirmation.

A lot of time, energy and just plain frustration are spent by minority students trying to adjust to the environment that exists on many predominantly White campuses. As a result, their academics suffer. Since these social factors directly impact on retention, they must be studied if institutions of higher learning expect meaningful progress in stemming the high attrition tide.

Institutional Racism

The truth is that racism exists throughout American society. Colleges and universities simply mirror that society. Institutional racism can be defined as discriminatory practices that have been internally adopted by an institution resulting in clear differences of treatment among people along racial lines. Sedlacek (1976) defines it as a pattern of collective behavior which results in negative outcomes for minorities. He has developed a six-step model suggesting ways in which racist behavior can be changed.

The struggle against racism must be waged by universties. Colleges have vast resources which if used properly could enable them to become agents for social change.

In looking at the enrollment decline at Berkeley back in the mid 70's Koon (1979) cited the leading reasons as racism and discrimination.

When academic pursuits take place in an atmosphere marred by racism the capacity of minority students to positively respond is seriously diminished. Campus life for minority students at predominately white campuses has always been difficult. For many students, institutional racism makes it impossible. Some indicators worth watching for that could serve as warning signals:

1. All white committees.

2. Absence of minorities (picture or print) in the campus press coverage.

3. Inflexible rules and guidelines that ignore the cultural needs of minority students.

4. Tokenism.

5. High attrition rates.

6. Using entrance exams based solely on white middle class culture.

7. Using text books that don't include the minority experience.

8. All white cultural environment.

Mono-Cultural Curriculum

The world is becoming increasingly non-White. By the year 2000 it is predicted that of the six billion people expected to populate the globe, five billion will be non-White. You wouldn't know that such a massive social phenomena exists by what's being presented in the classroom.

The prevailing pedogogical strategy is to teach about one culture only. The Indian learns that even his existence is questioned as students are taught that Columbus discovered America. Hispanics aren't told that Spanish settlements thrived in Texas, New Mexico and California long before the English colony of Jamestown existed. Asians helped to build the railroads that brought the east and west closer together, while on the back of Black slave labor, America's economy was saved. Given such a mono-cultural perspective it's not surprising that minorities learn their status in America is second class. It takes little imagination to figure out how people react when their existence is discussed as unimportant or completely ignored. Even when minority groups are presented it is often pathological or in a negative context, highlighting only the oppression and powerlessness of their people. This says a lot about the educational training and ideology of the classroom professor. Professors need to take a serious look at their bibliographic and reference materials for unilateral views. They should also widen their reading list to include Black and Hispanic authors.

Educators can analyze the relationship between course content and racism and pluralize their class presentations. If efforts such as these are not undertaken, white students (constantly bombarded with myths about white domination of each academic discipline) will continue to view themselves and their culture as superior to other groups. Such a view is extremely dangerous in a world where whites are the minority.

Even if a university does not have one minority student its curriculum and staff should be multicultural. Whites growing up in all white environments become culturally disadvantaged by their schools and may be woefully unprepared for the new emerging world order where an understanding and appreciation of cultural differences are necessary for peaceful coexistence.

There are several options available to institutions of higher learning serious about correcting this inequity.

A. One can teach the values of the dominant culture forcing the minority to adapt to the dominant society.

B. One can provide token acknowledgement of minority contributions; a page here, a paragraph there, Black History Week etc., or

C. One can implement cultural pluralism in which the minority experience is an integral part of the total curriculum. This latter course of action is preferred because America is not White. She is Brown, Black, Yellow, Red and White. The contributions of all of these people must be understood and taught. American Educational policy ought to reflect its populace.

Alienation

Socially, predominantly white universities are structured to meet white student needs. From fraternities to polka dancing, minority students find themselves outside the mainstream of college life.

A study conducted by Centra (1970) of eighty-three predominantly white institutions reveals a dual environment for Black students that leads to alienation. Suen (1983) confirmed that alienation leads to high attrition.

The college environment produces isolation and the psychological effects therefrom (Young, 1983).

Alienation creates an atmosphere of self doubt that makes interaction unbearable for some students. When you consider the low number of minority students enrolled, a situation exists in which there is often only one Black or one Indian in the classroom. These students often find themselves in an isolated position, obtaining little approval or support from their teacher or other students. Minority students are often left out of informal study groups, and have limited access to notes from past courses. Many find themselves on their own. The results show up in the high drop out rate.

Professor Expectations and Attitudes

The minority student is often viewed as an intellectual inferior and treated accordingly. Minority students report that professors expect less and often question completed assignments by them that are scholarly superior. Some students say that outside of the classroom, assistance is unavailable or given reluctantly.

This is not to suggest that all faculty are the same. There are many sensitive and caring teachers who experience success with minority students. However the professor is part of the larger system. As a result some of America's "learned" minds have never risen above the irrational notion of linking the ability to learn with one's race.

In large impersonal universities, instructors are rewarded more on their research abilities than on their teaching skills. Unfortunately this practice comes at the expense of all students.

Teachers play a decisive role in the retention chain. No improvement can be expected in decreasing the attrition rate without faculty leadership and involvement. There is a general concensus among researchers that academic achievement is highest for students who experience favorable faculty relations. Instructors can learn to understand that there is creativity and talent in minority communities. They can begin to expect excellence and use their influence to improve retention on campus.

Cultural Conflict

The minority student finds himself engulfed in white culture on most predominantly white campuses. Nearly everything he reads, hears, and sees reflect white values. The type of music, food, and social outlets he has in his community simply don't exist on many campuses.

College is a critical period in the development of a student's identity. It's the time when adolescence supposedly comes to an end. Students are eager to "fit in" and to be affirmed by their peers. There is evidence that minority students undergo a classic identity crisis that interferes with academic functioning, (Gibbs, 1974; Chickering, 1981).

When universities fail to provide cultural support the result is usually cultural conflict. This neglect frustrates students causing many to recoil into their own ethnic clubs and organizations.

Those all "Black" and "Chicano" tables present in many college unions and cafeterias serve a cultural reinforcement role in many respects, although they are for the most part depicted as supporting segregation. Some students argue that it is because of minority student organizations and cultural activities that they are able to survive the social life on predominantly white campuses.

Assessment Strategies

Probably no group on earth is more tested than American children. As David Nyberg (writing in the March 26, 1986 issue of the Chronicle of Higher Education) points out, the majority test out as "lacking in ability, aptitude or intelligence".

Does that tell us something about the majority of Americans or something about the majority of tests?

There has been considerable damage done to Blacks and Hispanics through improper testing. In 1969 the National Association of Black Psychologists (NABP) wrote a statement of support to parents who chose to defend their rights by refusing to allow their children to be subjected to standardized tests that are used to:

1. Label Black people as uneducable.

2. Place Black children in "special" classes and schools.

3. Perpetuate inferior education for Blacks.

4. Assign Black children to educational tracks.

5. Deny Black students higher education opportunities.

6. Destroy positive growth and development of black people.

In 1972 the NABP developed an even stronger position on testing calling for (among other things) *"legal action against standardized testing and a moratorium on the use of such tests until they are made culturally relevant,"*(Rivers, et,al 1975).

Brim, *et,al* (1969) estimates that millions of I.Q. tests are administered each year. They are administered by schools, colleges, the military, civil service, industry, etc. They are used for sorting, classifying, selecting, labeling, diagnosing and placement.

Perhaps the test that has caused the greatest consternation is the I.Q. test. It is used extensively for classification purposes. Definitions of intelligence are numerous. Generally speaking I.Q. tests are *"attempts to measure an individual's abilities and or skills"* (Ibid, p. 66). I.Q. and intelligence are not the same. The concept of I.Q. is derived from the formula MA/CA x100 where MA equals mental age and CA equals chronological age. Mental age, then is based on how well one answers items on the I.Q. test (Ibid, p. 66).

I.Q. tests are only valid if they can predict academic performance or predict future scores on future tests.

In discussing the limitations of such tests with the Black population we would highly recommend that you read Wendell Rivers article,"I.Q. Labels & Liability: Effects on the Black Child," in the Winter 1975 *Journal of Afro-American Issues.* Rivers and his colleagues consider six psychometric factors in building their case against the misuse of I.Q.

testing: 1) construct validity 2)concurrent validity 3) content validity 4) predictive validity 5) standardization and 6) reliability. They also speak to the dangers of misclassification and suggest alternatives to I.Q. testing.

They advocate for the discontinuation of such tests arguing that the tests have no validity or reliability for Blacks and other minority groups.

Another organization, Fair Test, Box 1272 Harvard Square Station, Cambridge, MA 02238 works with civil rights, consumer and other groups to educate the public about the uses and abuses of millions of standardized multiple-choice exams administered in the U.S. each year.

Universities evolved into their current obsession with test results as more efficient ways were required to determine who would gain admission. Even today the role that standardized tests play in determining admissions (especially in professional schools) is pervasive.

Given the overwhelming evidence supporting the notion of cultural biases in admissions tests, their continued use by colleges to exclude and label groups of people guarantee that minorities will be admitted less, receive less scholarships and have less graduate and job opportunities.

The use of standardized testing in admission policies serves to accomodate rather than rectify social and racial inequalities among higher education institutions.

Lack of Supportive Services

The fact remains that there are students who need extra help when they enter the university. There is no need to be apologetic in recognizing this need. Whenever social, educational, economic, political and cultural resources are unequal in the society the results are an advantaged status for some and a disadvantaged status for others.

Astin surveyed undergraduates at several hundred two and four year colleges and universities to find out why students drop out. He concluded the greatest predictive factor in retention was the student's past academic record and academic ability (Astin, 1975). This finding alone could justify remedial education.

In the academic year 1983-84, *"65% of institutions of higher education offered remedial mathematics instruction; 73% offered reading; and 71% offered writing. Of entering freshmen, 32 percent needed remediation in mathmatics, 27 percent in reading, and 28% in writing,"* (Wilson, 1985 p. 5).

It's not just a minority problem although a substantial number of minority students are effected. There is a substantial body of research that links the lack of supportive services to high attrition rates (Voyich, 1974). Many schools have responded by setting up "special" programs. According to Washington (1977) the following factors are key to survival and success of these programs: 1) institutional commitment 2) strong program leadership 3) support services 4) financial aid and 5) student commitment.

A problem that has to be addressed by special programs is the stigmatization many students feel by being associated with the program. Program planners must impress upon students the value of improving their academic skills. Students may need to spend up to 60 hours a week reading rather than the traditional 45 hours per week for 15 credits. When one is engaged in self improvement activity, stigmas are only temporary. Not being able to read or write is a far greater stigma than attending basic skill labs.

Socialization

Minority Student adjustment at predominantly white institutions often require that they adhere to white cultural norms rather quickly, ignoring their own cultural roots in the process. Orlando Taylor (1970) describes the university as a *"middle class entity that provides minority students inadequate provisions for cultural identity, psychological acceptance, feelings of relevance and achieving cultural goals".*

Others have found that students who adopted white middle class norms were more likely to experience success in higher education.

The process by which minority students are integrated into the social fabric of the institution causes many students to question the necessity of losing their ethnic identity in order to be accepted. Some students oppose assimilation on philosophical grounds arguing its time that minorities exercised social control of their lives.

While it's important for minority students to develop their own clubs and organizations, we believe it's a mistake for them not to participate in every aspect of college life, particularly those dealing with the establishment of policies and procedures governing student life and the disbursement of funds.

The research shows that students who get involved in campus activities generally do better in classes and increase their chances for persistence. Students who have developed interpersonal skills are usually better able to manipulate bureaucracies to their advantage.

Studies also indicate that minority students who've had positive interracial contact prior to college tend to experience more positive interracial contact on campus, (Bennett, 1984). It appears that black females experience a greater sense of frustration in socializing than black males. Dr. Fleming, (1984) warns of the alarming drop in social and assertive skills on the part of females. Add to that the depressing low number of males and you have a situation that's tenuous at best. A major change occurred in higher education from 1970-1983. There was a shift from a majority male enrollment to a majority female one.

Relevance

Just imagine if white and minority students were exposed to the great Black, Hispanic, Indian and Asian authors and scientists. Shakespeare may be alright but so is James Baldwin or Alex Haley. Greater interest can be created in the subject matter if students understand its meaning to their lives.

A math professor teaching students who were former migrant workers taught students how to figure out how many bushels of tomatoes had to be picked per day in order to pay the rent. A typing teacher had her class type an Indian alphabet and turned the students' reactions into a lesson. A chemistry teacher discussed the composition of hair products and informed students why most blacks need to oil their hair.

Professors must understand that they are working with a variety of students and cultures and that their charge is not so much to force everyone into the same mold as it is to give everyone the relevant tools for success. Minority students can be turned on to math if they are shown how it relates. They can be turned on to Shakespeare by changing "to be or not to be" to T.C.B or "tell it like it is".

One of the reasons for the Black college's success with Black students may be the feeling of relevance it offers Black students. In describing this feeling, Smith (1981) suggests that *"historically Black colleges have the unique ability to reach the unreachable, teach the unteachable, and embrace both the rejected and the valedictorians with equal concern."*

Motivation

With the previous nine social barriers facing minority students it is understandable that a lack of motivation is often present. Students can learn to view these problems not as crutches but rather as challenges. Studies have found that successful minorities tended to be independent, self assured and confident that they can change their lives by their own efforts. They expect racism and have prepared to deal with it. They have achieved some form of success outside the class room.

Jeanatte (1980) found a positive correlation between Indian students' positive self-concept of their Indian heritage and college success. Harris (1974) concluded that students who felt good about themselves and felt they had control over their lives would be more motivated to achieve in higher education.

The task for minority students on white campuses is not to retreat but to direct their anger and frustration into changing their educational environment. The greater the initiative students take to liberate themselves, the greater the improvement in their self esteem.

As a person develops a positive self-concept, he becomes more open to experience, does not need to distort the environment that he is perceiving, and thus can be more able to learn about himself. At the same time, since he/she is then able to receive stimuli from all sources with less distortion, experiencing his world more fully, he or she becomes more able to learn effectively in an academic setting, (Johnson, 1982).

Once students have developed a positive identity they are better able to direct their own lives. Institutions of higher learning can help students develop positive coping mechanisms.

Minority parents are beginning to understand that their sons and daughters must be prepared psychologically as well as academically to meet the demands of the learning environment at the college level. Parents therefore must be concerned with what they can do to improve motivational skills and in what ways the environment can be manipulated so that the student becomes excited about learning.

Strategies To Combat Negative Social Factors

1. Institutional racism

We would recommend a multicultural task force be created and charged with evaluating university policies in terms of bias. Start from the beginning-that is the type of contact that is made to get minority students to attend your campus and proceed to what is being or not being done to get minority alumni involved. Throughout your evaluation, keep asking what impact does this policy or practice have on minorities.

For equally serious acts of personal racism some campuses have established "hot lines" in which victims of racism can call for assistance or report racial incidents before they become major incidents.

2. Mono-Cultural Curriculum

We would recommend that your campus sponsor an institute on Curriculum Reform to share ways with faculty on how subject matter can be pluralized. Dr. Carl Grant professor of education at the University of Wisconsin-Madison has developed a model that allows almost any subject to be pluralized. Dr. James Banks professor at the University of Washington is perhaps the leading pioneer in multicultural education. His books and numerous articles are excellent starting points. We would also strongly recommend making ethnic studies courses mandatory.

3. Professor's expectations and attitudes

We would recommend annual workshops to sensitize faculty about the problems that minority students face. The workshops should inform faculty of the vital role they play in retention efforts. Some campuses have created a standing faculty committee on minority concerns. Others honor faculty at annual banquets for their exceptional work with minority students.

4. Cultural Conflict

We would recommend that minority cultural programs become an integral part of the student activities calendar. Speakers, films and musical events representing minority culture should be encouraged and integrated into the campus's social system. Some campuses have established "town-gown" committees to help students adjust to the community.

5. Assessment strategies

We would recommend that testing never be used as the sole criteria to deny a person access to a higher education. If your campus insists on using such tests in this manner we would urge that you check out the NAACP's successful coaching program that was used to improve black student performance on the S.A.T. Also Arnold Mitchum, former director of Marquette University's Educational Opportunity program has sponsored workshops on appropriate ways to use standardized tests with minority students. Finally we would refer you to Dr. William Sedlecek's (University of Maryland-College Park) NCQ instrument that often predicts the success rate of Black students better than the S.A.T.

6. Supportive Services

We would recommend linking existing supportive services with retention efforts by re-evaluating objectives in light of the findings discussed in this book. For those campuses with little or no existing supportive services it goes without saying that we would recommend creating such services based on Edward Chip Anderson's guidelines listed in the "Review of the Literature" section of this book.

7. Alienation

We would recommend that your institution engage in activities designed to make the environment welcoming. This can be done in part by pluralizing all media on campus, involving minority alumni as role models and hiring minority staff. Some campuses have created faculty mentor programs in which a faculty person is available to help students cope with a new environment.

8. Socialization

We would recommend that your campus establish an effective and appropriate orientation for minority students based on the guidelines included in the "Taylor Retention Model". Some campuses have experienced success by utilizing currently enrolled students in a variety of peer roles to make the "integration" process flow smoother.

9. Relevance

We would recommend that your campus offer culturally relevant programs such as black history college bowls, ethnic academic activities, multicultural instruction and analyze ways in which new perspectives can be introduced into the classroom resulting in meaningful education for all students.

10. Motivation

We would recommend your campus media run positive news stories about successful minority students. It's also important that minority students be exposed to leadership training and then placed in visible leadership roles on campus.

Summary

Given the nature of the social factors set forth on the previous pages it becomes apparent that an effective retention model needs to be global in its perspective. To some extent all students face these social factors, but only minority students face them in a compounded manner resulting in higher dropout rates for many in American higher education institutions. A supportive environment needs to become a top priority on many campuses. Such an environment lends itself to increased participation in activities, challenges students' intellects and helps in motivating them to achieve academically.

REVIEW OF THE LITERATURE

In preparing this book an ERIC Documents Search was initially conducted. It was soon revealed that there are literally several thousand articles and documents related to student recruitment, admission and retention. Narrowing the list down to only those with applicable information relating to Blacks and other Minorities still provided nearly two thousand documents. It was decided to emphasize those studies, books and articles that were published during the past ten years. Two documents from ERIC that guided this review proved to be extremely helpful. If your institution decides on a similar undertaking these two documents are highly recommended as a starting point:

ERIC document 228912 cites ways in which the literature conceives Black student retention, provides a detailed summary of factors affecting retention, and offers strategies and remedies (based on the research) to increase retention.

ERIC document 228911 includes over a hundred publications (1961-1982) on the retention of minority college students. The topics covered include: retention programs for low income and minority undergraduates; the interrelatedness of curriculum and cultural/economic reproduction; predicting academic performance in college, drop out prevention strategies and related topics.

The Journal of Negro Education dating from 1975-1985 proved invaluable. Entire issues have been devoted to persistence and comparisons of factors that have impact on retention.

The Ford Foundation has sponsored a number of studies and papers on the subject.

Dr. Jacequeline Flemming's book, *Blacks in College* offers additional insights.

Lee Noel's book, *Increasing Student Retention* (1985) is an excellent resource and is highly recommended.

Raymond Landis's book on *Improving the Retention and Graduation of Minorities in Engineering* (1985) offers an extremely helpful source of programs that work.

Howard University's Institution for the Study of Educational Policy has a good selection of papers suited to this topic. The National Advisory Committee on Black Higher Education and Black Colleges and Universities, before it was disbanded, had published well-researched studies dealing with an array of issues pertinent to attrition and retention.

Dr. Janet Wilson's study entitled *Wisconsin Indian Opinions of Factors Which Contribute to the Completion of College Degrees* offers a definitive look at factors contributing to successful Indian student persistence.

The author also reviewed hundreds of press releases from campuses that described innovative programmatic efforts.

Some additional Journals you may wish to review for pertinent information on the topic:

AAUP Bulletin

Alternative Higher Education

American Educational Research Journal

American Sociological Review

Bulletin of the Association of College Unions-International

College and University

College Press Review

College Student Journal

Community and Junior College Journal

Counseling and Values

ERIC Resources in Education

Educational Researcher

Higher Education

Human Relations

Improving College and University Teaching

Integrated Education

Journal of College Placement

Student Personnel

Journal of Consulting and Clinical Psychology

Journal of Counseling Psychology

Journal of Educational Psychology

Journal of Educational Research

Journal of Higher Education

Journal of Negro Education

Journal of Non-White Concerns in Personnel and Guidance

Journal of Student Financial Aid

Measurement and Evaluation in Guidance

NASPA Journal

Psychology Today

Sociology and Social Research

Youth and Society

Background

It has only been a relative short time (since the 60's) that minority students have been on predominantly white campuses in measurable numbers. Historically, by law or through practice, institutions of higher learning successfully kept minority students out of their doors. Since social movements culminating in civil rights gains rather than altruism are mainly responsible for increased minority student enrollments, perhaps it is not surprising that retention problems are the rule rather than the exception.

Retention issues gained a great deal of attention in the 70's. They will require even more if the problem of attrition is to be noticeably reduced.

Given this backdrop the literature approaches these concerns from several perspectives. This review will concentrate on two:

1) Factors that impact retention and

2) Strategies that have been adopted to improve retention rates of Minority students.

Factors Impacting Retention

Dr. Donald Smith's study (1980) identified several major barriers to minority student retention that the research tends to support:

1) Inadequate financial aid.

An example of this can be found in a study conducted by Axtel and Coad (1979) at Merritt College in Oakland, California. They found the leading reason for those students considering dropping out was financial difficulty. Most of the relevant research cited financial aid as the most significant factor in recruiting minority students, (Jones, 1979).

When the disproportionate number of minority students at or below the poverty level is taken into consideration, the lack of financial aid looms as a formidable barrier that threatens the limited gains that minority groups have made in higher education.

2) Feelings of alienation and loneliness.

Maurice Britts's book *Blacks on White College Campuses,* (1975) found that Minority students felt more alienated. Claerbaut (1978) confirms alienation experienced by Black students and offers a good conceptual view using such noted theorists as Marx, Weber and Durkheim.

The research supports alienation as a contributing factor at large predominantly white institutions as well as small private colleges. Smith and Baruch (1981) identified alienation and loneliness as the most common factors in Black student attrition expressed by students, Black faculty and administrators.

3) Failure to use available counseling.

It appears from the literature that minority students take less advantage of counseling services on campus than their white counterparts. The reasons for this remain unclear. Kaye (1972) found that required counseling improved grades and retention. Clark (1979) found that special counseling helped as well.

4) Inadequate secondary school preparation.

Poor preparation by incoming minority students was found to be a central determinant affecting student persistence by a number of authors (Bressler, 1967; Astin, 1971; Sowell, 1972; and Kowalski, 1977).

5) Cultural/racial identity adjustment.

Dr. Alvin Poussaint (1970) suggests that a realistic inability for meaningful self-assertion is a greater inhibitor of ability to achieve than other factors.

Gail Thomas's edited work, *Black Students in Higher Education, Conditions, and Experiences in the 1970's (1981)* chronicles the types of personal identity crisis and cultural conflicts minority students face on campus. The literature strongly implies that findings likeThomas's contributed to the Adams mandate with its goal of equal educational opportunity for black and minority students.

Literature from the 60's to the mid 70's noted numerous attitudinal conflicts and warned of increases in racially based dissention on campus. Contemporary studies confirms the importance of racially distinquishable attitudinal conflicts as they relate to attrition.

These attitudinal conflicts are important to keep in mind when taking a historical look back at minority student arrival at predominately white campuses. For example during the 60's the primary goal was "integration". Minority students were expected to fit into white structures. White models were used to mold black student behavior. Taylor (1970) criticizing the educational system, suggested that Black students be educated on terms that respect and accommodate their cultural differences. A number of Black and Hispanic educators demanded that the cultural needs of minority students be addressed.

Miscellaneous Factors

Additional factors impacting retention that the literature cites includes sexual/social relationships. Glenny, (1980) predicts an increase in the number of minority college students during and following the 80's. Presently Black females outnumber Black males. In institutions of higher learning with increased interracial dating, primarily on the male's part this factor may loom more significant in the years ahead.

Other studies identify such factors as family socioeconomic status, motivation, values, self esteem, and environmental characteristics as influencing student attrition, (Bressler, 1967; Reed, 1978; Axtel and Coad, 1979; Burlew, 1979; Harrower et al., 1980; Lenning, Beal, and Sauer, 1980; Smith, and Baruch, 1981).

Strategies to Improve Retention
(Identified by the literature)

The "Action Plan for the California Community Colleges" (California Community Colleges, 1979), points to four strategies for positively affecting minority student retention. These four strategies include:

1) expanded efforts in outreach, recruitment, and admissions;

2) responsive and sensitive counseling, student services, and basic skills support;

3) greater development of support services and special programs; and

4) improved faculty, staff and student awareness of underrepresented students and their preferred modes of learning.

The literature provides a wide selection of programs and activities that fall into the above mentioned strategies.

1. Expanded Efforts in Outreach
There appears to be a general consensus that universities which make genuine efforts in the form of pre-collegiate, targeted admissions and enrichment programs experience greater success with retention than those who don't (Astin, 1978; Anderson, 1978; Boyd, 1974; and Cope, 1975).

2. More Responsive and Sensitive Counseling
The literature points to the need for appropriate counseling at the high school as well as the collegiate level. Through effective counseling students are made aware of course requirements and services on campus that will assist them in successfully completing their tenure. Through responsive counseling, students' awareness of the possibilities open to them are expanded and they are given assistance in reaching the types of decisions necessary for them to choose options compatible with their talents and goals.

An approach considered effective was identified by (Crockett, 1978). Other researchers have cited career planning and counseling as a strategy affecting retention (Kaye, 1972; Hillery, 1978).

3. Greater Development of Support Services

Although developed in 1978, Edward "Chip" Anderson's eleven themes (used to guide retention programs for minority undergraduates at UCLA) still appear to be timely and supported by the literature. They can be found in a Chapter entitled "A Retention Design Applied to an Equal Opportunity Program", in Lee Noel's book *Reducing the Dropout Rate*.

The themes are listed below:

1) Program goals must be endorsed and supported by the institution's officials, and programmatic activities must be consistent with these goals. The goals which Anderson lists as requiring administrative endorsement and support include: (a) the desired mix of students to be recruited, and admitted; (b) the level of academic performance desired from the various groups of students recruited, admitted, and retained; and (c) the rate of persistence expected and desired among the student groups.

2) Retention should begin with an ethically conducted recruitment program based upon documented characteristics of persisters.

3) To improve the flow of nontraditional students into colleges, alliances should be formed with feeder high schools and community colleges.

4) Institutions should offer a thorough orientation, such that students understand institutional demands.

5) It is important for participants to identify with equal opportunity programs yet not feel stigmatized by them.

6) The best retention services directly address areas of greatest student anxiety and frustration (i.e., financial resources, academic skills deficiencies, lack of career plans, difficulty in adjusting to the campus).

7) Retention programs should take the initiative in promoting and providing services.

8) In order to ensure program relevance, students should be treated equally as consumers.

9) Campus support for an equal opportunity program will result if the program accomplishes its objectives and demonstrates its value to the institution.

10) It is necessary to have an effective staff able to re-late to students-a staff which can serve as change agents to stimulate student persistence and performance.

11) Program management must develop a developmental perspective.

Anderson's themes tend to draw a great deal of support from the literature as recommended strategies (Boyd, 1974; Washington, 1977; Clark, 1979; Romano, 1980; Zanoni, 1980; and Mohr, 1981).

4. Improved faculty, staff and student awareness

Approaches that involve the faculty in retention efforts seem to experience the most success, (Spady, 1971; Fisher, 1978; Walton, 1979; Harrower, et al., 1980). The presence of Black faculty to serve as role models was seen to have a positive effect on Black Students retention in both integrated and Black Schools, (Fleming, 1984). Peer support was cited as a major factor associated with persistence in college, (Haagen, 1977).

The literature supports strategies that address both
academic and social concerns, (Tinto, 1975; Cope, 1978). In
addition, the integration of academic and social concerns is
offered as a strategy to improve faculty awareness of minority
students culture and to improve understanding on how cultural
differences influence learning, (Young, 1981).

Summary

Each of the four approaches mentioned above
should be viewed as relational. In conjuction with each other
they present an effective approach to the problem of retention.
If universities adopt them as strategies, the literature strongly
suggests that their efforts will meet with success.

To summarize, a review of the literature indicates that
over the past ten to twenty years a growing body of research
has developed that provides a better picture of collegiate experiences in dealing with retention. The research identifies a
number of independent variables, many of which we've high-
lighted in this book. Although there are effective strategies
that work on some campuses, the research does not identify
one model or one strategy that would be applicable to all
situations. However the research does tend to strongly
support the notion of a holistic approach. It is on this
premise that the Taylor Minority Student Retention Model is
based.

Future Research Needs

What became clear in the review of the literature was
the lack of any definitive approach that would answer the
question, *"What makes for a successful Minority College Student?"* It does seem obvious that both institutional and personal factors play a role in Minority Student attrition rates.
Future research must analyze these two perspectives more
thoroughly. It may be equally important to study Black-Black
and Black and other minority retention differences and causes.

This is an area that has received little attention and may in the long run provide meaningful data and useful strategies that could assist campus administrators in ways that contemporary Black-White research comparisons cannot. Future research should also look into the ten questions posed by Dr. Stephen J. Wright, a consultant for the College Entrance Examination Board and former President of Fisk University in a lecture delivered at Howard University, Nov 5, 1980 and published in the *Journal of Negro Education* Vol 50, No.2 (1981). Substituting the word Black for Hispanic and Indian will give meaning to the notion that these are concerns shared by all minorities.

1. What are the differences-educational, psychological, social and economic between Black high school dropouts and those who persist, and how can urban schools be more responsive to these differences?

2. What special counseling needs do children from seriously disadvantaged educational and economic backgrounds need and where in the educational process should it seriously begin?

3. What are the major contributing factors for the relatively poor performance of Blacks on standardized tests, with special reference to admissions tests?

4. What special educational problems, if any, are generated by life in ghetto communities?

5. What special educational problems, if any, typically develop in homes of low socio-economic status?

6. How are motivation and self-concepts developed in children from seriously disadvantaged backgrounds?

7. What are the critical elements in those public schools in ghetto communities that manage to help pupils over come disadvantagement and move at normal rates of achievement?

8. What are the really critical componentsof college developmental programs that can help students over come serious academic disadvantages?

9. What are the specific barriers that keep the number of Blacks from admission to and the successful pursuit of graduate and professional study low?

10. What changes, if any, are needed in financial aid programs that would further reduce the financial barriers to higher education?

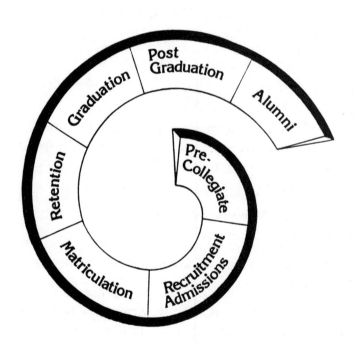

INITIATIVES WORTH CONSIDERING

The issues that we've discussed and the retention model we've presented in this book will hopefully provide discussion and direction as to how campuses, communities, individuals and private industry can become involved in ways that do make a difference.

By following the recommendations we've suggested, by studying what other campuses have done and internalizing it locally, campuses can experience improved results.

In order to stimulate your thinking and to get you started on an action plan we have provided some initiatives for your consideration. Some have received a forum nationally, others may be new ideas. In combination with what has already been presented they should prove useful.

A. University and University System's Administrative Initiatives

It's important that state higher educational systems establish some consistent minimum standards (conformity) and a coordinated approach, while at the same time allowing for creativity and local autonomy. If state systems adopted the retention model introduced in this book, institutions could be required to offer programs in each of the areas included in the model while still being allowed the flexibility of establishing innovative programs that are "proper and adequate" for their campus.

Other programmatic ideas worth considering:

-Sponsoring a statewide, regional or national conference to brainstorm and address the issue of recruitment and retention.

-Encouraging early identification and intervention of Minority student academic problems.

-Working with your state's Voc-Tech boards, Department of Public Instruction and other state funding agencies to better coordinate pre-collegiate opportunities.

-Creating special visiting (rotating) minority professorship positions.

-Requesting a system-wide study of the loan debt faced by minority students and requesting appropriate recommendations to reduce the loan debt to comparable levels faced by white students.

-Sponsoring system wide workshops and in-service training on recruitment, retention and social factors faced by minority students.

-Contracting with minority owned consultants/businesses to address problems in this area.

-Requesting a study of what happens to the 30-60% of minority students who drop out prior to graduation.

-Requiring yearly evaluations of recruitment and retention efforts.

B. Department of Public Instruction (DPI) Intitatives

Campuses won't be able to resolve the retention problem alone. They will need to establish strong linkages with their state's department of public instruction to make sure elementary and secondary schools perform their responsibilities as well. Here are some things DPI's can do:

-Sponsor minority student leadership conferences, aimed at providing students with the skills and incentives needed to pursue a higher education.

-Work with Vocational Technical boards to contract with inner city community based organizations to develop drop-out prevention programs and basic skill laboratories for high school drop outs.

-Provide funding for university-middle school outreach programs.

-Provide workshops for middle and high school counselors.

-Sponsor a statewide essay contest for high school students on "How students would handle the drop-out problem".

-Sponsor statewide inservices providing teachers with effective strategies to use when working with multicultural populations.

-Work with the state legislature to establish incentives for school districts to improve their minority student retention rates.

-Provide summer science, math and computer camps for middle and high school youngsters.

-Provide annual data on the number of minorities placed in special education classes; the drop-out rate and the suspension rate drawing attention to these problems and providing appropriate action to decrease these rates.

C. Legislative Initiatives

When you view the problems that minority students are having on our campuses with the problems minorities are having in the larger society, you can't ignore the political causes and effects. In a very real sense, part of the solution to the retention dilemma lies within the political process. If state and federal governments continue to be remiss in adequately addressing the needs of minority education, even the best attempts by educators to turn things around may fall short of the desired goal.

Legislative remedies could play a leading role in increasing educational access and retention. A recent study cited three major contentions for legislative involvement:

(1) "Increased federal and state legislative involvement in the education of minorities must take place to facilitate greater achievement by blacks; (2) the nature of legislative involvement necessitates major changes in some already existing programs and (3) increased legislative involvement should be in the form of a series of formal incentives aimed at motivating

teachers and administrators to better educate and facilitate the academic needs of minority students. These incentives include those of an economic nature that would be directly provided to teachers, individual schools and districts," (Brown, 1981).

Since 1954, the federal government has taken its educational responsibilities somewhat seriously, culminating in a Department of Education under former president Jimmy Carter. Unfortunately the Reagan administration appeared determined to destroy many of the gains the educational community had made. With the weight of higher educational opportunities now shifting to the states, for minority educational programs to maintain the limited progress they've made is to depend on new leadership from state legislatures. As a result here are some things state legislatures can do:

-Pass appropriate legislation that allows for increasing financial flexibility in the school aid formula for districts with concentrations of low income students.

-Pass appropriate legislation that requires DPI and Vocational Technical agencies to work with minority community based organizations in attacking the minority high school drop-out problem. Encourage joint state agency planning to view minority retention problems from a global perspective and earmark resources from various state agencies.

-Provide additional funding for minority support programs, out-of-state tuition remissions, precollegiate programs and attempt to work out tuition reciprocity agreements with states sending large numbers of minority students to yours for education.

-Provide legislation that assesses penalties and provides for enforceable authority in making sure universities implement their affirmative action plans.

-Encourage state supported vocational/technical schools to develop satelite programs and linkages in the minority community.

-Develop youth initiative programs.

-Create a special Minority Education sub-committee task force to advise the Legislative Education Committee on these issues.

-Serve as a model on the state and federal level in terms of hiring a multicultural staff.

-Vote to increase financial aid generally and grants specifically for low income students.

-Work to increase funding for black colleges. The amount of funding they receive from the federal government contrasted with the task they've been performing indicates a pattern of benign neglect.

-Designate a portion of revenue sharing monies for the improvement of the quality of life for minority children.

D. Private Industry Initiatives

Clearly the private sector has a stake in minority education. The minority community represents this country's future workforce. The investment private industry devotes to this segment of our society could have enormous payoffs in the long run. Here are some things private industry can do:

-Donate computer software and hardware for student training.

-Sponsor apprenticeship, internship, and training programs in the minority community.

-Help coordinate and fund scholarship programs for minority students.

-Adopt a public school with a high concentration of minority students.

-Initiate Sponsor a Youth (S.A.Y.) programs for high school and college students.

-Write "empowering" contracts with the minority community enabling individuals to own franchises and businesses leading to greater economic development.

-Hire and promote minority graduates.

-Provide "on-loan" executives to work with high schools to help motivate students to explore the math and science fields.

E. Minority Community Initiatives

The community's stake in all of this can't be underestimated. During our research for this book we observed dozens of campuses located in the hearts of cities with little ties to the minority community. Recruiting and retaining students can only be done with, not in isolation to the minority community. On the other hand, minority communities shouldn't wait to be asked for assistance. Institutions of higher learning tend to be more receptive to criticism of their efforts when the groups doing the criticizing are also pitching in to resolve the difficulties. As a result here are some things minority communities can do:

-Conduct "Stay In School" campaigns.

-Get involved with local school boards and local schools as advocates for minority students.

-"Adopt" minority students new to your community that are attending college and get them involved in the community.

-Sponsor Town-Gown minority community orientation nights.

-Help coordinate scholarship fundraising drives.

-Monitor research activities that are state and federally funded which impact the lives of minority children.

-Encourage minority scientists to develop evaluative instruments to measure the strength and talents of minority children.

-Expose children to examples of excellence.

-Help foster independence, not dependence in children.

-Join alumni associations and take an active interest in college affairs.

F. Minority Student Initiatives

-Network with student organizations and share strategies that work in keeping students in school.

-Conduct community workshops on the benefits and opportunities of a college education for minority youngsters.

-Study hard while in school and strive to achieve academically which means homework done well, classes attended, reports finished and preparations for class accomplished.

-Get involved in campus activities and work to make the environment accomodating to minority student needs.

-Assist with campus recruitment and retention efforts.

-Organize to protect your own cultural, political and economic interests.

-Work for more ethnic courses, minority faculty, increased minority student enrollment and more financial assistance.

The ball is in the minority student's court. It's important that students understand past sacrifices and struggles that enabled many to attend predominantly white institutions. With such an understanding there remains the possibility of a permanent vanguard looking out for the educational interests of future generations of minority students.

CONCLUSION
_____

What follows are a set of indicators supported by research findings related to the recruitment and retention of Minority Students:

- An institution's special recruitment efforts to attract minority students do lead to increased minority admissions.

- Admission standards have not been lowered as a result of Affirmative Action activities.

- The level of a student's academic preparation plays a central role in determining a student's persistence but his/her chances for success can be improved with remedial education.

- Alienation along with financial difficulty appear to be the leading causes for high minority attrition.

- Strategies that include outreach efforts, strong support services and sensitive faculty have a positive affect on retention.

- Financial Aid is apparently the most significant factor when recruiting minority students.

- High school grades predict minority student success better than standardized tests or high school rank. College grades are even better predictors.

- Special services aimed specifically at minority students are more effective at increasing retention than services designed for all students.

- Programs addressing social factors, student anxieties and frustrations, and environmental issues have a positive impact on minority retention rates.

- Increased state and federal legislative involvement in minority education (in the form of economic incentives) helps to increase achievement in retention programs.

- Social interaction with faculty has a positive impact on minority retention.

This book represents our contribution to the recruitment and retention predicament. We have attempted to build a case demonstrating that an effective retention program is comprehensive and global. The program your campus adopts must be institutionalized and generate involvement from the total campus to experience lasting gains.

Many of the recommendations we've included don't require additional funding or personnel. Others call for the reallocation of existing funds and services. All of them require leadership and a humanistic approach to the problem.

Recent changes in minority enrollment can be used as a gauge to tell us how this country is responding to its citizens who have the greatest educational needs. Another equally important reason for studying minority recruitment and retention is to see if our universities are becoming more plural or merely widening the gap between whites and minority groups.

On the basis of the evidence it has been estimated that the years 1964 to 1974 were the golden age of educational opportunities for blacks. Nearly 50,000 new Black students enrolled in college each year from 1965-73.

If colleges are to maintain and surpass those figures in the foreseeable future they will need to implement programs and activities similar to the ones we've recommended. By doing so institutions can push America to come to terms with its dream of equal opportunity for all.

Let's go forward with hope, but as we do, remember to keep in mind that results, not intentions must continue to be the yardstick to measure progress.

Bibliography

ACE Research Reports. "The Black Student in American Colleges." Vol. 4, No.2 Office of Research, Council on Education, 1969.

Adenike, T.J., and Berry, G.L. "Teachers Attitudes Toward the Education of the Black Child." *Education*, 97 pp. 102-114, 1967.

Albach, Philip G., and Berdahl, Robert. *Higher Education in American Society.* Buffalo: Prometheus Books, 1981.

Anderson, Edward "Chip". "A Retention Design Applied to an Equal Opportunity Program." In Lee Noel (Ed.), *Reducing the Dropout Rate.* San Francisco: Jossey-Bass, Inc., 1978.

Anderson, Arnold C. "Education and Social Change." *School Review*, 1972 80 (3) 433-458.

Astin, Alexander W., Fuller, Bruce, and Green, Kenneth C. (Eds) *Admitting and Assisting Students after Bakke.* San Francisco: Jossey-Bass, Inc. 1978.

Astin, Alexander W. *Minorities in American Higher Education: Final Report of the Commission on Higher Education of Minorities.* San Francisco: Jossey-Bass, 1982.

-- *Predicting Academic Performance in College; Selectivity Data for 2,300 American Colleges.* New York: The Free Press, 1971.

-- *Preventing Students from Dropping Out.* San Francisco: Jossey-Bass, Inc. 1975.

Astin, Alexander W. *The College Environment.* Washington, D.C.: American Council on Education, 1968.

Ausubel, David. "The Effects of Cultural Deprivation on Learning Patterns." *Audiovisual Instruction,* 10: 10-12, January, 1965.

Axtel, Dayton and Coad, Alison. *A Study of a Sample of Merritt College Students: Reasons precipitating possible withdrawal, and attitude toward service and instruction.* No 11. Oakland, California: Northern California Community Colleges Research Group, 1979, (Eric Document Reproduction Service No ED 186047).

Bailey, Robert. *Minority Admissions*. Lexington, MA: Lexington Books, 1978.

Baker, G. "Multicultural Imperatives for Curriculum Development in Teacher Education." *Journal of Research and Development in Education,* Fall 1977, p.70-83.

Ballard, Allen B. *The Education of Black Folk.* New York: Harper Row, 1973.

Bandura, Albert, and Huston, Aletha C. "Identification as a Process of Incidental Learning." *Journal of Abnormal and Social Psychology,* 63 (1961): 33-318.

Banks, J.A. "Social Problems and Educational Equity in the Eighties." (Eric Document Reproduction Service No Ed 220366), 1981.

Barzun, Jaques. *Race: A Study in Superstition.* New York: Harper and Row, 1965. (First Published in 1937).

Beal, Philip E., and Noel, Lee. *What Works in Student Retention.* Iowa City, Iowa: The American College Testing Program and National Center for Higher Education Management Systems, 1980.

Benedict, Ruth. *Race, Science and Politics*. New York: Viking Press, 1943.

Bennett, Christine "Interracial Contact Experience and Attrition among Black Undergraduates at a Predominantly White University." *Theory and Research in Social Education:* v12 n2 p.19-47 (Summer 1984).

Biddis, M. *Father of Racist Ideology: The Social and Political Thought of Count Gobineau.* New York: Weinright and Talley, 1970.

Blackwell, James E. *Mainstreaming Outsiders: The Production of Black Professionals.* Bayside, N.Y.: General Hall, 1981.

Blakely, B.E. *Alumni Administration at State Colleges and Universities. An Analysis of Current Perspective and Practices in Alumni Administration: The Results of a National Survey.* Washington, D.C.: Council for Advancement and Support of Education, 1979.

Bloom, Benjamin S. "Mastery Learning." Chapter 4 in *Mastery Learning Theory and Practice,* James H. Block (Ed.) New York: Holt, Rinehart and Winston, 1971.

Bluedog, K., and Kittson, D. A legal position paper on Indian Education. *In Compendium Report to Congress from the National Advisory Council on Indian Education,* Las Cruces, NM: ERIC/CRESS,1981.

Blyden, Edward W. *Christianity, Islam, and the Negro.* London: Edinburg University Press, 1967. (First Published in 1887).

Bond, Arthur J., Lebold, William K. *Factors Associated with Attracting and Retaining Black Americans in Engineering.* Washington, D.C.: American Society for Engineering Education, 1977. (ERIC Document Reproduction Service No. ED 176602).

Bowles, Samuel. "Getting Nowhere: Programmed Class Stagnation." *Social Science and Modern Society* , 1972 9 (8), 42-48.

Bowles, Samuel, and Gintis, Herbert. *I.Q. in the N.S. Class Structure: Power and Ideology in Education,* (Ed.), Jermone Karabel and A.H. Halsey, New York, Oxford Press, 1977.

Boyd, William M. *Desegregating America's Colleges, A Nationwide Survey of Black Students,* 1972-73. New York: Praeger Publishers,1974.

-- "The Forgotten Side of the Black Undergraduate: An Assessment of Academic Achievements and Aspirations During the 1970's", in G. Thomas, (Ed.), *Black Students in Higher Education: Conditions and Experiences in the 1970's.* Westport, Conn., Greenwood, 1981, pp. 142-151.

Braddock, Jomills. *"The Major Field Choices and Occupational Career Orientations of Black and White College Students",* in G. Thomas, (Ed.), *Black Students in Higher Education: Conditions and Experiences in the 1970's.* Westport, Conn., Greenwood, 1981, pp. 167-184.

Braithwaite, Ronald L. *Hampton Institute Alumni Census--Final Report,* Hampton Institute, VA.: Educational Resources Center, December, 1978.

Bressler, Marvin. "White Colleges and Negro Higher Education." *Journal of Negro Education,* 26 (Summer 1967): 258-65.

Brim, O. G.; Glass, J. Neulinger; I. J. Fireston and S. C. Lerner. *American Beliefs and Attitudes About Intelligence,* New York: Tussell Sage Foundation, 1969.

Britts, Maurice W. *Blacks on White College Campuses.* Minneapolis: Challenge Production Inc., 1975.

Brown, Frank. "Legislative Remedies for Increasing the Educational Access and Retention of Minorities." In Gail E. Thomas (Ed.), *Black Students in Higher Education, Conditions and Experience in the 1970's.* Westport, Connecticut: Greenwood Press, 1981.

Brown, Nicholas C. *Orientation to College Learning-A Reappraisal,* American Council on Education, Washington, D.C., 1961.

Brunson, F. Ward. "Creative Teaching of the Culturally Disadvantaged." *Audiovisual Instruction.* 10, 30, January, 1965.

Buffalohead, R. *Higher Education of Indian Students; 200 years of Indian Education.* Tempe, AZ: Center for Indian Education, Arizona State Univ., 1976.

Buffkins, Archie. "White Students at Black Schools." *Journal of Afro-American Issues,* 5 (Winter, 1977): 66-71.

Bumpas, D.E. and Roger L. Gordon. "Bridging the Gulf for the Disadvantaged", *Audiovisual Instruction.* 12:442-45, (May, 1967).

Burlew, Kathleen Hoard. "Black Youth and Higher Education. A Longitutinal Study." Ohio: 1979. (ERIC Document Reproduction Service, No. Ed 181 100).

California Assembly Office of Research. "Dropping Out, Losing Out: The High Cost for California." Sacramento, CA: Joint Publications Office, 1985.

California Community Colleges, Sacramento Board of Governors, *Action Plan for the California Community Colleges,* 1979. (ERIC Document Reproduction Service No. ED 192 822).

California Postsecondary Education Commission, *The Resource Directory of California Equal Educational Opportunity and Student Affirmative Action Programs, 1981-1982.* Long Beach and Sacramento, California, 1982. This directory provides a comprehensive list of California programs involved with equal educational opportunities at the postsecondary level.

Catterall, J. S. "On the Social Costs of Dropping Out of School." Stanford, California: Institute for Research on Education, 1986.

Colvin, Deltha. "Reagan's FY'85 Budget to Reduce Programs for the Disadvantaged Student", *National Minority Campus Chronicle.* Vol 2, (11) (April, 1984).

Carey, Philip; Singh, Balslave; and Pillinger, Barbara. "Impact: a Summer Enrichment Program for Minority Disadvantaged Undergraduates at the University of Minnesota." In Gail E. Thomas (Ed.), *Black Students in Higher Education Conditions and Experiences in the 1970S.* Westport, Connecticut: Greenwood Press, 1981.

Carnoy, M. *Education as Cultural Imperialism.* New York: McKay, 1974.

-- "Education, Democracy and Social Conflict", *Harvard Educational Review, 1983* 53 (4) 398-402.

Catteral, James S. "Dropping Out." UCLA Graduate School of Education, Volume 4, Number 1 Spring, 1986.

Centra, John A. "Black Students at Predominally White Colleges: A Research Description." *Sociology of Education,* 43 (Summer 1970) 325-39.

Centra John A. "College Enrollment in the 1980's, Projections and Possibilities." *Journal of Higher Education,* 51 (January February, 1980): 18-39.

Chase, Allen. *The Legacy of Malthus: The Social Costs of the New Scientific Racism.* New York: A. Knoph, 1977.

Chase, C.E. and Johnson, J.J. "Predicting College Success with Nontraditional Data for Inner-City Students."*Journal of College Student Personnel,* 18 (May, 1977), 210-214.

Chickering, A.W. and Associates. *The Modern American College: Responding to the New Reality of Diverse Students and a Changing Society.* San Francisco, Jossey-Bass, 1981.

Claerbaut, David, P. *Black Student Alienation: A Study.* San Francisco: R & E Research Associates, Inc., 1978.

Clark, Kenneth. *Dark Ghetto.* New York: Harper & Row, 1965.

Clark, Robert M. " Special Counseling Study, Fall, 1978, Entering Class." California: Reedley College, 1979. (ERIC Document Reproduction Service No. Ed 175 498).

Cleary, T. Anne. "Test Bias: Prediction of Grades of Negro and White Students in Integrated Colleges." *Journal of Educational Measurement,* 5, 1968, pp. 115-124.

Cohen, Robert D., and Ruth, Jody. *Freshman Seminar: A New Orientation.* Boulder, CO Westview Press, 1978.

Coleman, J.S.; Blum A.D.; Sorenson, A.B.; and Rossi, P.H. "White and Black Careers During the First Decade of Labor Force Experience; Part I: Occupational Status." *Social Science Research,* 243-270, 1972.

College Entrance Examination Board, "Trends in Student Aid: 1980-1984." Washington, D.C. 1984, p.2.

Combs, A., Soper, D., and Courson, C. "The Measurement of Self-Concept and Self-Report." *Educational and Psychological Measurement,* 23 (1963), 493-500.

Cope, Robert G. "Why Students Stay, Why they Leave." In Lee Noel (Ed), *Reducing the Dropout Rate.* San Francisco: Jossey-Bass Inc., 1978.

Cope, Robert G., and Hannah, William. *Revolving College Doors: The Causes and Consequences of Dropping out, Stopping Out, and Transferring.* New York: Wiley, 1975.

Council, Kathryn A. *Graduation and Attrition of Black Students at North Carolina State University, Raleigh, North Carolina.* North Carolina State University, Division of Student Affairs, 1974 (Eric Document Reproduction Service No.ED 130 588).

Cox, Archibald. "Minority Admission After Bakke." *In Bakke, Weber, and Affirmative Action.* Working papers from a Rockfeller Foundation Conference, July 12-13, 1979. New York: The Rockfeller Foundation, 1979.

Cox, George O. *African Empires and Civilizations.* Washington, D.C., African Heritage Studies Publishers, 1974.

Crim, Alonza A. "Technology for Pre-Service and In-Service Training of Teachers of Ghetto Children." (ERIC Document Reproduction Service. No. ED 039 739), 1970.

Crockett, David S. "Academic Advising: Cornerstone of Student Retention." In Lee Noel (Ed.), *Reducing the Dropout Rate.* San Francisco: Jossey-Bass, Inc. 1978.

Cross, Patricia H., and Astin, Helen. "Factors Affecting Black Students' Persistence in College." In Gail E. Thomas (Ed.) *Black Students in Higher Education, Conditions and Experiences in the 1970s.* Westport, Connecticut: Greenwood Press, 1981.

Crossland, Fred E. *Minority Access to College.* New York: Schacker Books, 1971.

Cutts, Warren G. "Special Language Problems of the Culturally Deprived." *Clearinghouse.* 37: 80 3 (October, 1962).

Daves, Samuel C., Loeb, Jane W., and Robinson, Lehymann F. "A Comparison of Characteristics of Negro and White College Freshman Classmates." *Journal of Negro Education.* 39 (Fall 1970): 359-66.

Davis, J.A., and Temp, G. "Is the SAT Biased Against Black Students?" *College Board Review.* Fall, No. 81, p. 4-9, 1971.

Davis, William G., Welty, Gordon A. American College Personnel Association, Oberlin College, Ohio, Princeton University N.J. "The Old System and the New College Students." (ERIC Document Reproductive Services ED 038 707), 1970.

Deskins, Jr., Donald R. "Minority Recruitment Data: A Preliminary Report." Racham Reports, University of Michigan, 7, 2 (1981), 1-5.

Dicesare, Anthony C., et al. "Non-Intellective Correlates of Black Student Attrition." College Park, Maryland: University of Maryland Cultural Study Center, 1970. (ERIC Document Reproduction Service. No ED 049 714).

Digest of Educational Statistics. US. Dept. of Education. Office of Educational Research and Improvement, 1988.

Diop, C.A. *The Cultural Unity of Black Africa.* Chicago: Third World Press, 1978.

Dusek, J.B. "Do Teachers Bias Children's Learning? *Review of Educational Research.* 1975 45, 661-684.

Dunston, F. Myron, and others. "Review of the Literature: Black Student Retention in Higher Education Institutions." (ERIC Document Reproductive Services ED 228 912), 1983.

Dunston, F. Myron, and others. "Annotated Bibliography: Black Student Retention in Higher Education Institutions." (ERIC Document Reproductive Services ED 228 911), 1983.

Eaton, C. *Freedom-of-Thought, Struggle in the Old South.* New York: Harper Torchbook, 1964.

Eckland, Bruce K., and Wisenbaker, Joseph M. *National Longitudinal Study: a Capsule Description of Young Adults Four and one-half years After High School.* Research Triangle Institute, February 1979.

Etzioni, Amitai. *The Active Society.* New York: The Free Press, (1968).

Fanon, F. *A Dying Colonialism.* New York: Evergreen, 1965.

--   *Black Skin, White Masks.* New York: Grove, 1967.

Fisher, James L. "College Retention From a Presidential Perspective." In Lee Noel (Ed.), *Reducing the Dropout Rate.* San Francisco: Jossey-Bass, Inc., 1978.

Fleming, J. "Special Needs of Blacks and Other Minorities." in A.W. Chickering (Ed.) *The Modern American College.* San Francisco: Josse-Bass, (1981).

Fleming, J. *Blacks in College.* San Francisco: Jossey Bass Publishers, 1984.

Francher, Evelyn P. "Educational Technology: A Black Perspective." (Eric Document Reproduction Service. No ED 240 213), 1983.

Friere, Paulo. *Education for Critical Consciousness.* New York: Seabury, 1973.

Gamson, William A. *Power and Discontent.* Homewood, Illinois: Dorsey, 1968.

Garrett, H. E. *Heredity: The Cause of Racial Differences in Intelligence.* Kilmarnock, VA: Patrick Henry Press, 1971.

Gibbs, J. T. "Black Students/White University: Different Expectations." *Personnel and Guidance Journal.* 1973, 51, 463-469.

Gibbs, J. T. "Patterns of Adaptation Among Black Students at a Predominantly White University." *American Journal of Orthopsychiatry.* 1974, 44, 728-740.

-- "Use of Mental Health Services by Black Students at a Predominantly White University: A Three-year Study" *American Journal of Orthopsyschiatry.* 1975, 45, 430-445.

Gibby, R. G. and Gabler, R. "The Self-Concept of Negro and White Children." *Journal of Clinical Psychology.* XXIII ,1967, 144-148.

Ginzburg, Eli. "Black Power and Student Unrest: Reflection on Columbia and Harlem." *The George Washington Law Review.* 33 (May 1969) 835-47.

Glennen , Robert E. "Intrusive College Counseling." *College Student Journal.* (February/March, 1975), 2-4.

Glenny, Lyman A. "Demographic and Related Issues for Higher Education in the 1980s". *Journal of Higher Education.* 51 (July/ August 1980) 363-380.

Godard, James M. *Educational Factors Related to Federal Criteria for the Desegregation of Public Postsecondary Education.* Atlanta: Southern Regional Education Board, 1980.

Goodrich, A. *A Data Driven Model for Minorities in Predominantly White Institutions* .(Paper presented at the National Conference on Advising, Vermont, 1977).

Goodrich, A. *A Data-Driven Retention Model for Improving Minority Student Persistence in Higher Education Institutions.* Chicago: Data-Driven Retention Systems Ltd., 1980.

Goodrich, A. "New Programs and Services for Higher Education's New Student." *Journal of Afro-American Issues.* 5 (Winter, 1977) 20-32.

Gosman, Erica J., and others. *Predicting Student Progression: The Influence of Race and other students and Institutional Characteristics on College Students Performance.* AIR Forum 1982.

Green, D. R. *Racial and Ethnic Bias in Test Construction.* Monterey, California, McGraw-Hill, 1972.

Gurin, Patricia and Epps, Edgar G. *Black Consciousness, Identity and Achievement.* New York: Wiley, 1975.

Haagen C. Hess. *Venturing Beyond the Campus: Students who leave College.* Middletown, Connecticut: Wesleyan University Press, 1977.

Hahn, Ralph W. "In Defense of Dropping out: A Forthright Refutation of Community College Dogma." *Community College Review* . (Winter, 1974) 35-40.

Hall, E.T. *Beyond Culture.* New York: Anchor (1977).

Hamilton, Charles V. "On Affirmative Action as Public Policy." *In Bakke, Weber, and Affirmative Action.* Working papers from a Rockfeller Foundation Conference, July 12-13, 1979. New York: The Rockfeller Foundation, 1979.

Harris, L. *Characteristics of Self-Regard, Locus of Control and Academic Achievement of Selected American Indian Students in Higher Education.* (Doctoral Dissertation, University of Washington, 1974).

Harrower, Gordon, Jr., Herrling, John R., Houpt, Ann, Maugle, Kenneth B. "Retention: An Inductive Study of Representative Student Groups at Middlesex County College." Edison, New Jersey Middlesex County College 1980, (ERIC Document Reproduction Service. No. ED 198 851), 1980.

Haynes, Leonard L. "The Adams Mandate: A format for Achieving Equal Educational Opportunity and Attainment." In Gail E.Thomas (Ed.), *Black Students in Higher Education, Conditions and Experience in the 1970s.* Westport, Connecticut: Greenwood Press, 1981.

Hedegard, James M. and Brown, Donald R. "Encounters of Some Negro and White Freshman with a Public Multiversity. *Journal of Social Issues.* 25 (summer 1969) : 131-44.

Henderson, Cathy. *Changes in Enrollments by 1985.* Policy Analysis Service Report, Vol. III, No 1. Washington, D.C.: American Council on Education, 1977.

-Henderson, C., and Plummer, J. C. Adapting to Changes in the Characteristics of College Age Youth, Policy Analysis Service Reports, 4 (2), Washington, D.C.: American Council on Education, 1978.

Hilgard, Ernest R, and Bower, Gordon H. "Learning and the Technology of Instruction," Chapter 16 in *Theories of Learning* 3rd (Ed.) New York: Appleton-Century-Crafts, 1966.

Hilliard, Asa D. *Anatomy and Dynamics of Oppression.* An address delivered at the first national conference on Human Relations in Education. June 20, 1978.

Hilliard, Asa D. "Equal Educational Opportunity and Quality Education." *Anthropology and Education Quarterly.* September 2, 1978, pp.110-126.

-- "The Education of Inner-City Children." *Demythologizing the Inner City Child.* R.C. Granger and J. Young (Eds.) Washington, D.C.: National Association for the Education of Young Children, 1976.

Hillery, Milton C. "Maintaining Enrollments Through Career Planning." *New Directions for Students Services.* 3 (1978) : 13-22.

Hodge, J.L., Struckmen, D.K., and Frost L.D. *Cultural Bases for Racism and Group Oppression: An Examination of Traditional "Western" Concepts, Values, and Institutional Structures which Support Racism, Sexism, and Elitism.* Berkeley: Two Riders Press, 1975.

Hraba, J. and Grant, G. "Black is Beautiful: A Re-examination of Racial Preference and Identification." *Journal of Personality and Social Psychology.* XVI, (Nov., 1979), 398-402.

Hyde, William D. Jr. (Ed.). "The Effect of Tuition and Financial Aid on Access and Choice in Postsecondary Education." In *Issues in Postsecondary Education Finance.* Summaries of Six Issues Report No. F78-2, Education Commission of the States. (June, 1978), pp. 28-35.

Jackley, Janet P., and Henderson, Cathy. *Retention: Tactic for the Eighties.* Washington, D. C.: American Council on Education, December, 1979.

James, George M. *Stolen Legacy.* San Francisco: Julian Richardson, 1976.

Jaynes, William E. and others. *Alumni Attitudes: Men and women's Description of Their College Experiences, Present work and Present Recreational Activities.* (Paper presented to the annual meeting of the Southwestern Psychological Association, 1981).

Jeanotte, L.D. *A Study of the Contributing Factors Relating to Why American Indian Students Dropout of or Graduate from Educational Programs at the University of North Dakota.* (Doctoral Dissertation, 1980).

Jenks, Christopher. *Inequality: Reassessment of the Effects of Family and Schooling in America.* Basic Books, 1972.

Jensen, Arthur. "How much can we boost I. Q. and Scholastic achievement? *Harvard Educational Review.* 1969.

Johnson, Sylvia T. "Dimensions of the Self-Concept in Inner City Children", *Journal of Negro Education.* Vol. 51 No.4, 1982.

Jones, Larry G. *Black Students Enrolled in White Colleges and Universities: Their Attitudes and Perceptions.* Atlanta, Georgia: Southern Regional Education Board, 1979. (ERIC Document Reproduction Service No. ED. 181 834), 1979.

Jordan, V. E. Jr. "Blacks in Higher Education: Some Reflections." *Daedalus.* 1975, 104, 160-165.

Kaye, Robert A. "A Required Counseling Study Skills Program for Failing College Freshman." *Journal of College Student Personnel* . (March 1972) " 159-162.

Kelsall, R.K. and Poole, Anne, and Kuhn, Annette. *Graduates: The Sociology of an Elite.* London: Methuen & Co. Ltd., 1972.

King, Kenneth J. *Pan Africanism and Education: A Study of Race, Philanthropy and Education in the Southern States of America and East Africa.* Oxford: Clarendon Press, 1971.

Komoski, P. K. "4xE= Equitable Electronic Educational Excellence," (ERIC Document Reproduction Service. No. ED 239 377), 1983.

Koon, Jeff. "Undergraduate and Graduate Enrollments of Black and Chicanos at UC-Berkeley": University of California, (ERIC Document Reproduction Service. No. ED 180 425), 1979.

Kowalski, C., *The Impact of College on Persisting and Nonpersisting Students.* New York: Philosophical Library, 1977.

Larson, Richard and James L. Olson. "A Method of Identifying Culturally Deprived Kindergarten Children," *Exceptional Children.* 30: 130-4, (Nov., 1963).

Lazerson, Marvin (essay review of) "Social class, Ethnicity and Education in American History." *Harvard Educational Review.* 1982 52 (3).

Leary, M.E. "Children Who are Tested in an Alien Language: Mentally retarded?" *The New Republic.* 162(22), 17-18, 1970.

Leggett, Glen. "The Small Private College and Equilibrium Between Change and Constant Values." *Centennial Review.* 14 (Winter 1970) 1-16.

Lenning, Oscar T., Beal, Philip E., and Sauer, Ken. *Retention and Attrition: Evidence for Action and Research.* Boulder. Colorado: National Center for Higher Education Management System, 1980.

Levin, Henry M. "Federal Grants and Educational Equity." *Harvard Educational Review.* 1982, 52 (3) 441-448.

Levin, Henry M. "The Cost ot the Nation of Inadequate Education." Report to the Select Committee on Equal Educational Opportunity, U.S. Senate. Washington, D.C.: U.S. Government Printing Office, 1972.

Lincoln, C. Eric. "In the Wake of Bakke." In *Bakke, Weber, and Affirmative Action*. Working papers from a Rockefeller Foundation Conference, July 12-13, 1979. New York: The Rockfeller Foundation, 1979.

MacDonald, Kenneth E., and Sites, Paul. *Attitudes Toward Various Conceptions of Black Power Among Black and White University Freshmen.* Paper presented at the 67th Annual Meeting of the American Sociological Association, New Orleans, Louisiana, 1972.

Mann, Dale. "Educational Policy Analysis and the Rent-A-Troika Business." (ERIC Document Reproduction Service. No ED 207 228), 1981.

Martin, John Henry. "Technology and the Education of the Disadvantaged," (ERIC Document Reproduction Service. No ED 031 293), 1968.

Mather, Anne D. "University-Wide Planning for the Minority Student." *Regional Spotlight.* Vol. IX, No. 3. Atlanta, Georgia: Southern Regional Education Board, 1975. (Eric Document Reproduction Service No ED 149 663).

Mayhew, Lewis B. *Surviving the Eighties: Strategies and Procedures for Solving Fiscal and Enrollment Problems.* San Francisco: Jossey-Bass, Inc. 1979.

Mays, B.E. "The Black College in Higher Education." In C.V. Willie and R.R. Edmonds (Eds), *Black Colleges in America.* New York: Teacher College Press, 1978.

Memmi, Albert. *The Colonizer and the Colonized.* Boston: Beacon Press, 1968.

Mercer, J.R. "I.Q. The lethal label." *Psychology Today.* Sept., 6, 46, 1972.

Messick.W., Anderson, S. "Educational Testing, Individual Development and Social Responsibility." *The Counseling Psychologist.* 2 (2): 993-97, 1970.

Minugh, C. *Continuing College Education: A Guide for Counseling the American Indian Student.* ERIC/CRESS, Las Cruces, New Mexico, 1982.

Moen, Norman W. (Ed.) "Renovation of the A.A. Degree Program: The General College Retention (PEP) Program Evalution of General College." *General College Newsletter.* 26, May 1980. ERIC Document Reproduction Service, No. ED. 190 1976.

Mohr, Sr., Paul B. "Issues Related to Affirmative Action: Policies and Programs for Admission and Retention of Minority Students." *The Negro Educational Review.* Vol. XXXII, No.1, Jan. 1981.

Montaza, A. *Man's Most Dangerous Myth: The Fallacy of Race.* New York: Oxford University Press, 1974.

Montaza, A. *The Concept of Race.* New York: Collier, 1964.

Morris, Lorenzo. *Elusive Equality: The Status of Black Americans in Higher Education.* Washington, DC: Howard University Press, 1979.

National Advisory Committee on Black Higher Education and Black Colleges and Universities, *Access of Black Americans to Higher Education: How Open Is the Door?* Washington, D.C.: Government Printing Office, 1979.

Nettles, Michael T. Gosman, Erica J; Dandridge, Betty; and Theony, Robert A. "The Desegregation of Higher Education; An Analysis of the Influence of Race on student Progress and Attrition," unpublished, March, 1982 in Reginald Wilson's *Fourth Annual Status Report, Minorities in Higher Education.* American Council on Education, 1985.

Newlon, L .L., and Gaither, G. H. "Factors Contributing to Attrition: An Analysis of Program Impact on Persistence Pattern." *College and University.* 55 No 2 (1980) 235-251.

Nieves, Louis. *The Minority College Experience: A Review of the Literature.* Princeton: Educational Testing Services, 1977.

Noel, Lee. "First Steps in Starting a Campus Retention Program." In Lee Noel (Ed.), *Reducing the Dropout Rate.* San Francisco: Jossey-Bass, Inc., 1978.

Noel, Lee, and Beal, Philip E. *Reducing the Dropout Rate: Campus Level Retention Strategies and Action Program.* Iowa City, Iowa: The ACT National Center for Educational Conference, 1979.

Noel, Lee, Levitz, Randy S., Saluri, Diana, and associates. *Increasing Student Retention.* San Francisco: Jossey-Bass, 1985.

Ogbu, John U. *Minority Education and Caste.* New York: Academic Press, 1978.

Ott, Linda. "Admissions Management with the Focus on Retention." In Lee Noel (Ed.), *Reducing the Dropout Rate.* San Francisco: Jossey-Bass, Inc.,1978.

Owen, David *None of the Above* (*Behind the Myth of Scholastic Aptitude).* Boston, Houghton Mifflin Company, 1985.

Pantages, Timothy J., and Creedon, Carol F. "Studies of College Attrition: 1950-1975." *Review of Educational Research.* 48 (Winter,1978) 49-101.

Pearce, R.H., *Savagism and Civilization.* Baltimore: The Johns Hopkins Press, 1965.

Peng, Samuel S. and Fetters, William B. *College Student Withdrawal: A Motivational Problem.* Research Triangle Park, North Carolina Research Triangle Institute, 1977,   (ERIC Document Reproduction Service No. ED 148 206).

Persell, Caroline H. *Education and Inequality: The Roots and Results of Stratification   in America's Schools.* New York: The Free Press, 1977.

Peterson, Marvin, W., Blackburn, Robert T., Gammson, Xelda F.. Arce, Carlos H., Davenport, Roselle W., and Mingle, James R. *Black Students on White Campuses; The Impact of Increased Black Enrollments.* Ann Arbor: Institute for Social Research, The University of Michigan, 1978.

Pettigrew, Thomas F. "The Effects of the Bakke Decision: An Initial Look." In *Bakke, Weber, and Affirmative Action.* Working papers from a Rockfeller Foundation Conference, July 12-13, 1979. New York: The Rockefeller Foundation, 1979.

Pfeifer, C.M. and Sedlacek, W.E. "Predicting Black Student Grades with Nonintellectual Measures." *Journal of Negro Education.* 43, (1974), 67-76.

Poussaint, Alvin F., and Akinson, Carolyn. "Black Youth and Motivation." *Black Scholar.* 1970 Vol 1, No. 5, p 43-51.

Press Releases were edited from dozens of Universities and used in this book.

Rawles, Beth. "The Media and its Effect on Black Images", (ERIC Document Reproduction Service, No ED 158 300), 1975.

Reed, Rodney J. "Increasing the Opportunities for Black Students in Higher Education." *The Journal of Negro Education*. 47 (1978): 143-150.

Renter, Lois. "College Student Retention: An Annotated Bibliography." In Lee Noel (Ed.), *Reducing the Dropout Rate*. San Francisco: Jossey-Bass, Inc., 1978.

Report of the White House Conference on Children. Washington, D.C.: Government Printing Office, 1970.

Riessman, Frank. *The Culturally Deprived Child*. New York: Harper and Row, 1962.

Rivers, Wendell L., and Mitchell, Horace, and Williams, Willie S. "I.Q. Labels and Liability: Effects on the Black Child." *Journal of Afro-American Issues*. Vol. 3-No.1, (Winter, 1975).

Rodney, Walter. *How Europe Underdeveloped Africa*. Washington, D.C.: Howard University Press, 1974.

Romano, Joan L., and Garfield, Joan B. *A Curricula Experiment for Underprepared Minority Students: An Evaluation of the General College Pilot Educational Packages*. Minneapolis: University of Minnesota, 1980. (ERIC Document Reproduction Service No. 195 213).

Rooney, Jr., John F. *The Recruiting Game: Toward a New System of Intercollegiate Sports*. Lincoln: University of Nebraska Press, 1980.

Rootman, Irving. "Voluntary Withdrawal From a Total Adult Socialization Organization: A Model." *Sociology of Education*. 45 (1972) 258-270.

Rose, James R. "Some Plain Talk on Retention by a College Dean." In Lee Noel (Ed.), *Reducing the Dropout Rate*. San Francisco: Jossey-Bass, Inc., 1978.

Sanford, Timothy B. *Non-Academic Factors, Influencing the "Withdrawal" of Academically Ineligible Black Students.* Chapel Hill: University of North Carolina, 1979. (ERIC Document Reproduction Service No. Ed 180 362).

Samkanze, S. *Origins of Rhodesia.* New York: Praeger, 1969.

Schludermann, S. and Schludermann, E. "Personality Correlation of Adolescent Self-Concepts and Security-Insecurity." *Journal of Psychology.* LXX (1970), 85-90.

Scott, Gloria Randle. "The Economic Future: Institutional and Student Financial Aid for Blacks in Higher Education." In Gail E. Thomas (Ed)., *Black Students in Higher Education Conditions and experience in the 1970s.* Westport, Connecticut: Greenwood Press, 1981.

Sedlacek, William E., and Brooks, Glenwood C., Jr. *Racism in American Education: A Model for Change.* Chicago: Nelson-Hall, 1976.

Sedlacek, W.E. "Issues in Predicting Black Students Success in Higher Education." *Journal of Negro Education.* 43 (1974), 512-516.

Sedlacek, William E., and Webster, Dennis W. *Admissions and Retention of Minority Students in Large Universities.* College Park, Maryland: University of Maryland, Counseling Center, 1977, (ERIC Document Reproduction Service No. ED 139 889).

Sewell, William. "Inequality of Opportunity for Higher Education." *American Sociological Review.* 36 (October 1971), 793-809.

Seymour, Harold J. *Designs for Fund Raising.* New York: McGraw Hill, 1966.

Shapiro, H. Svi. "Education and the State in Capitalist Society: Aspects of the Sociology of Nico Poulanatias."*Harvard Educational Review.* 1980 50 (3) 320-325.

Silberman, Charles E. *Crisis in the Classroom.* New York: Vintage Books, 1971.

Silverstein, Barry and Krate, Ronald. *Children of the Dark Ghetto.* New York: Praeger Publisher, 1975.

Simmons, Wilber D. *Survey and Analysis of Higher Education Programs for the Disadvantaged Student.* U.S. Dept. of HEW, 1970.

Simpkins, G., Gunnings, T. and Kearney, A. "The Black Six-Hour Retarded Child" *Journal of Non-White Concerns in Personnel and Guidance.* Vol. 2, No. 1, October , 1973.

Skinner, B. F. "Reinforcement Today." *American Psychologist.* Vol 13, No.9, 1958.

Sindler, Allan P. *Bakke, Defunis and Minority Admissions: The Quest for Equal Opportunity.* New York: Longman, 1978.

Smith, Donald H., and Baruch, Bernard M. "Social and Academic Environments on White Campuses. *Journal of Negro Education.* 50, No.3 (1981) 299-306.

-- *Admission and Retention Problems of Black Students at Seven Predominantly White Universities.* Washington, D.C.: National Advisory Committee on Black Higher Education and Black Colleges and Universities, 1980.

Smith, Noel T., Maxwell, Jack D., Carney, Myrna L., Fontaine, Phyllis D. "Student Retention Studied." *College and University.* 51 (1976) 652-654.

Sowell, Thomas. *Black Education-Myths and Tragedies.* New York: David McKay Company, Inc. 1972.

Spaeth, Joe L., and M. Greeley, Andrew. *Alumni Reactions to College Student Protest.* Chicago: National Opinion Research Center. February, 1970.

Spady, W. "Dropout From Higher Education: Toward an Empirical Model." *Interchange.* 2 (1971): 38-62.

Spring, Joel, *American Education: An Introduction to Social and Political Aspects.* New York: Longman Inc, 1982.

Stanfield, James D. "Socioeconomics Status as Related to Aptitude, Attrition, and Achievement of College Students. *Sociology of Education.* Vol 46, Fall, 1973.

Stone, Winifred V. "Mood of the Black Student on the Predominantly White Campus." *Journal of Afro-American Issue*. (Winter 1977) 4-18.

Suen, Hoi K. "Alienation and Attrition of Black College Students on a Predominately White Campus." *Journal of College Student Personnel*. v24 n2 p. 117-21 (March, 1983).

Tabata, I. B. *Education for Barbarism in South Africa: Bantu (Apartheid) Education*. London: Pall Mall Press, 1960.

Taylor, Orlando L. "New Directions for American Education: A Black Perspective." *Journal of Black Studies*. 1 (September, 1970): 101-12.

Thomas, A., and Sillen, S. *Racism and Psychiatry*. New York: Brunner Mazel, 1972.

Thomas, C. L., and Stanley, J. C. "The Effectiveness of High School Grades for Predicting College Grades of Black Students, A Review and Discussion." *Journal of Educational Measurement*. VI (1969), 203-215.

Thomas, Gail E. "The Future of Blacks in Higher Education: Recommendations and Conclusion." In Thomas, (Ed.), *Black Students in Higher Education, Conditions and Experiences in the 1970s*. Westport, Connecticut: Greenwood Press, 1981.

--   "The Effects of Standardized Achievement Test Performance and Family Status on Black-White College Access." In Thomas (Ed.), *Black Students in Higher Education, Conditions, and Experiences in the 1970s*. Westport, Connecticut: Greenwood Press, 1981.

Thompson, R. A. and Cimbolic, P. "Black Students' Counselor Preference and Attitudes Toward Counseling Center Use." *Journal of Counseling Psychology*. 1978, 25 (November) pp. 570-575.

Thorndike, E. L. *Educational Psychology*. New York Teacher College, Columbia University, 1913.

Tilton, Betty D. *The Development and Use of a Computerized Data Base for Monitoring Student Retention*. Tallahassee, Florida: AIR Forum, University of Minnesota. (ERIC Document Reproduction Service No. ED 174 097), 1979.

Tinto, Vincent. "Dropout From Higher Education: A Theoretical Synthesis of Recent Research." *Review of Educational Research.* 45 (1975) 89-125.

Turner, B. A. "Ten Years of Success at Minority Recruitment." *Engineering Education.* 64 (7) p. 528-530, April 1974.

Voyich, D. L. *A Study of Selected Characteristics of Successful and Unsuccessful American Indian Students Enrolled at Montana State University from September 1967 to June 1972* . Doctoral Dissertation, Montana State University, 1974.

Wade, Serena E. "Media and the Disadvantaged - A Review of the Literature." (ERIC Document Reproduction Service No ED 027 741), 1969.

Wagner, Thielens, Jr. "Undergraduate Definitions of Learning from Teachers." *Sociology of Education Journal.* 50 (July, 1977), 159-181.

Walton, Joseph M. "Retention, Role Modeling, and Academic Readiness: A Perspective on the Ethnic Minority Student in Higher Education."*The Personnel and Guidance Journal.* (October 1979): 124-127.

Washington, K.R. "Special Minority Programs: Dupe or New Deal?" *Journal of Afro-American issues.* 5, (Winter 1977): 60-65.

Webster, D.W., Sedlacek, W.E., and Miyares, J. "A Comparsion of Problems Perceived by Minority and White University Students." *Journal of College Student Personnel.* 20 (March 1979), 167-170.

Weinreich, M. *Hitler's Professors: The Part of Scholarship in Germany's Crimes Against the Jewish People.* New York: YIVO, 1949.

Welch, Finis. "Black-White Differences in Returns to Schooling." *American Economic Review.* 63 (December 1973), 893-907.

Wesman, A.G. "Intelligence Testing." *American Psychologist.* (4), 267-274, 1968.

Williams, Chancellor. *The Destruction of Black Civilization.* Chicago: Third World Press, 1974.

Williams, R. L. "Scientific Racism and I.Q.: Silent Mugging of the Black Community." *Psychology Today.* Vol. 7, No.12, pp.32-41, 1974.

Willie, C.V. and A.S. McCord. *Black Students at White Colleges.* New York: Prager Press, 1973.

Wilson, Janet G. *Wisconsin Indian Opinions of Factors which Contribute to the Completion of College Degrees.* Madison, Wisconsin: Wisconsin Center for Education Research, June 1983.

Wilson, Reginald, and Melendez, Sarah E. *Fourth Annual Status Report 1985, Minorities in Higher Education.* American Council on Education, 1985.

Woodson, Carter G. *Miseducation of the Negro.* Washington. D.C.: Associated Publishers, 1969. (First published in 1933).

Young, Herman A. "Retaining Blacks in Science: An Affective Model." In Gail E. Thomas (Ed.), *Black Students in Higher Education, Conditions and Experiences in the 1970s.* Westport, Connecticut: Greenwood Press, 1981.

Young, Herman A. "Cultural Differences that Affect Retention of Minority Students on Predominately White Campuses." (ERIC Document Reproduction Service ED 233 100), 1983.

Zanoni, Candido P. *The 1979-80 General College Retention Program, Final Report: Pilot Education Program.* Minneapolis: University of Minnesota, (ERIC Document Reproduction Service No. Ed 195 2120), 1980.

MINORITY STUDENT SERVICES DELIVERY SYSTEM
SELF-EVALUATION INSTRUMENT

Based on numerous discussions with campus administrators and individuals interested in evaluating their minority student services delivery system, we have created an instrument to allow campuses to take a comprehensive look at the services they provide minority students.

This instrument allows you to perform a self evaluation on minority student programs offered by your campus. The program areas included for evaluation make up what the research cites and campus administrators of successful programs cite as necessary for effective ways to recruit and retain minority students.

This instrument permits seventeen critical program area components to be evaluated ranging from pre-collegiate activities, the freshman year, faculty involvement to overall retention efforts. This evaluation tool provides the framework for assessing institutional committment to minorities. It should help you to answer questions like:

How do we determine priorities in our delivery system?

Where in the delivery system are we the strongest? the weakest?

Instructions

Examples of activities that are generally found in successful programs are provided for each program area discussed.

Next to each activity listed rank your institution's current efforts. For those activities listed that are absent from your campus write in <u>O</u> for not applicable. Likewise if your campus offers activities not listed fill in the <u>other</u> section. At the end of each program area you're asked to prioritize each.

You're also asked to evaluate each area in terms of effectiveness. These two rankings along with the discussion questions provided will assist you in targeting future retention efforts.

1. Pre-Collegiate

This program area includes all those activities your institution does to get minority youngsters thinking about college at an early age and involved in an actual collegiate experience while still in elementary or secondary school.

Pre-Collegiate Issues

Use this scale to complete your ranking

Not Applicable	Inadequate	Fair	Good	Excellent
0	1	2	3	4

Pre-Collegiate Activity   Ranking

a) College for Kids (elementary & middle school level)type programs offered   _____

b) Academic programs for high school students offered   _____

c) Upward Bound type programs offered where students actually live on campus, take college courses, etc.   _____

d) Potential students told what high school courses are needed for college admission   _____

e) Linkages established with elementary and secondary schools   _____

f) Other _____   _____
            fill in

g) Keeping in mind the seventeen retention program areas included in this self evaluation instrument where do you feel that pre-collegiate activities should be placed in terms of priority/resources?

Circle One

0	1 2 3 4 5 6	7 8 9 10 11 12	13 14 15 16 17
unable to answer	high priority	average priority	low priority

h) How effective are your current Pre-Collegiate efforts?

Circle One

0	1 2 3	4 5 6	7 8
unable to answer	ineffective	adequate	very effective

Discussion Questions:

-What type of contact should we establish with minority students in elementary and secondary schools?
-What role if any should our institution play in addressing the high minority student dropout rate in high school?
-What type of objectives do we need to establish to ensure that our pre-collegiate activities enhance our retention efforts?
-In what ways might we involve minority parents in our pre-collegiate activities?

Comments:

2. Recruitment

This program area includes all those activities your institution engages in to identify potential minority students.

Minority Student Recruitment

Use this scale to complete your ranking

Not Applicable Inadequate   fair   Good Excellent
    0   1   2   3   4

Activity   Ranking

a) Minority student marketing plan developed/
implemented   _____

b) Adequate recruiting budget established   _____

c) Personal contact given to potential students _____

d) Minority networking links developed   _____

e) Feeder high schools identified   _____

f) Summer bridge programs established   _____

g) Minority students currently enrolled involved in
recruiting   _____

h) Students invited to campus prior to admission _____

i) Follow up activities offered   _____

Activity	Ranking

j) Alumni involved in recruitment efforts of students
 in their localities

         _____

k) Other _____   _____
                    fill in

l) Keeping in mind the seventeen retention program areas included in this self evaluation instrument, where do you feel
recruitment activities should be placed in terms of priority/
resources?

Circle One

0	1 2 3 4 5 6	7 8 9 10 11 12	13 14 15 16 17
unable to answer	high priority	average priority	low priority

m) How effective are your current recruitment efforts?

Circle One

0	1 2 3	4 5 6	7 8
unable to answer	ineffective	adequate	very effective

Discussion Questions:

-From what sources both traditional and non-traditional are
minority students identified?
-What has proven to be our most successful strategy in recruiting Black students? Hispanics? Indians? and Asians?
-How many new minority students annually represent transfer
students and what type of institutions are they transferring
from?

-Do we have a comprehensive minority student marketing plan in place with an adequate budget that will allow it to work?
-How is the entire university involved with recruitment?
-What type of monitoring system do we need to install for those disciplines with a relatively low number of minority students?

Comments:

3. Admissions

This program area includes all those activities your institution engages in to increase the actual numbers of minority students admitted.

Use this scale to complete your ranking

0	1	2	3	4
not applicable	inadequate	fair	good	excellent

Activity   **Ranking**

a) Application form easy to complete/inviting   _____

b) Statistics kept on minority students contacted, admitted and actual shows   _____

c) Non-cognitive factors considered in admissions process   _____

d) Standardized test scores alone aren't used to disqualify students   _____

Activity	Ranking

e) Flexible admissions policy in place for borderline students _____

f) Follow up done on late applicants _____

g) Minority representation/input on admission committees and policy _____

h) Minority admission goals and timetables established as guidelines _____

i) Other _____ _____

                        fill in

j) Keeping in mind the seventeen retention program areas included in this self evaluation instrument where do you feel that admission activities should be placed in terms of priority/ resources?

Circle One

0	1 2 3 4 5 6	7 8 9 10 11 12	13 14 15 16 17
unable to answer	high priority	average priority	low priority

k) How effective are your current admission efforts?

Circle One

0	1 2 3	4 5 6	7 8
unable to answer	ineffective	adequate	very effective

Discussion Questions:

-What type of goals and timetables need to be established to guide our admission plans?

-How does our tuition costs and financial aid resources impact our admission rates of minority students?

-What type of linkages and working arrangements need to be established between the admission office and various academic and student support services on campus?

-Do we need to rethink our admissions operations from that of a sales oriented approach to one of a management oriented approach?

-Should we establish an alumni admissions program in several cities?

-What non-cognitive factors should we give added weight to, in the admissions process?

-Does the data we collect provide us with accurate enrollment information?

-How does the percentage of minority students admitted under normal admissions criteria contrast with the percentage admitted under special criteria?

Comments:

4. Matriculation

This program area includes all those activities your institution engages in once the admission process is complete, up to the first day of class.

Use this scale to complete your ranking

0	1	2	3	4
not applicable	inadequate	fair	good	excellent

Activity   **Ranking**

a) Students informed about support services
available on campus   _____

b) Students given effective advising enabling them
to enroll in appropriate classes   _____

c) Student housing needs are met   _____

d) Student financial needs are met   _____

e) Students placement tests are monitored ensuring
they've completed all necessary tests   _____

f) Students are provided a tour of the campus   _____

g) Students are given an orientation to the non-
collegiate community   _____

h) Other _____   _____
                        fill in

i) Keeping in mind the seventeen retention program areas included in this self evaluation instrument, where do you feel that matriculation activities should be placed in terms of priority/resources?

Circle One

0	1 2 3 4 5 6	7 8 9 10 11 12	13 14 15 16 17
unable to answer	high priority	average priority	low priority

j) How effective are your current matriculation efforts?

Circle One

0	1 2 3	4 5 6	7 8
unable to answer	ineffective	adequate	very effective

Discussion Questions:

-Do we have information on those minority students admitted who fail to enroll and why?
What type of follow-up is made to those minority students who have been admitted prior to the start of class?
-Are our students' housing, financial aid and academic advising needs taken care of before class begins?

Comments:

Retention

This program area represents the foundation of a campus's total efforts. It picks up where matriculation ends and includes: Orientation, The Freshman Year, Financial Aid, Academic Advising, Counseling/Career Development, Learning Resource Center, Faculty Involvement, Student Incentives, Social Factors and Affirmative Action activities.

5. Orientation

A good orientation program represents a vital link in the retention chain. Students in general find campuses perplexing. That's why an orientation program is critical, because it's often the first encounter a minority student has with that campus.

Use this scale to complete your ranking

0	1	2	3	4
not applicable	inadequate	fair	good	excellent

Activity	Ranking
a) Orientation Director or committee monitors orientation activities	_____
b) Orientation provided in a year long course	_____
c) Orientation involves parents	_____
d) Student-faculty interaction encouraged	_____
e) Upper class persons involved in orientation	_____

f) Other _____ _____
                    fill in

g) Where do you feel that orientation activities should be placed in terms of priority/resources?

Circle One

    0   1 2 3 4 5 6   7 8 9 10 11 12   13 14 15 16 17
unable to   high priority   average priority   low priority
answer

h) How effective are your overall orientation efforts?

Circle One

    0   1 2 3   4 5 6   7 8
unable to   ineffective   adequate   very effective
answer

Discussion Questions:

-In what ways is the orientation experience integrated with academic services and programs?
-How has the university prepared to receive minority students?
-What factors should we consider before adopting a semester or year long orientation course?
-Should we consider a separate minority student orientation in addition to the regular orientation?
-How do the objectives established for our orientation program contribute to retention?

Comments:

---

6. The Freshman Year

One factor that is becoming increasingly common in the retention literature is the impact the freshman year has on student persistence. Schools who have found success in decreasing high dropout rates generally have targeted special attention to their freshman class.

Use this scale to complete your ranking

0	1	2	3	4
not applicable	inadequate	fair	good	excellent

Activity   **Ranking**

a) Creative scheduling used so that minority
students aren't isolated in class rooms   °   _____

b) Freshmen year targeted for special activities   _____

c) Freshmen made to feel part of a community   _____

d) Freshman hour/course offered that stresses study
skills, team building, cultural acclimation and positive
self esteem   _____

e) Other _____   _____
                        fill in

f) Where do you feel that the Freshman Year activities should be placed in terms of priority/resources?

Circle One

0	1 2 3 4 5 6	7 8 9 10 11 12	13 14 15 16 17
unable to answer	high priority	average priority	low priority

g) How effective are your current Freshmen Year efforts?

Circle One

0	1 2 3	4 5 6	7 8
unable to answer	ineffective	adequate	very effective

Discussion Questions:

-What types of intervention strategies and programs should we administer during the freshman year to increase the retention rate?
-What steps might we take to reduce in-class attrition on the part of freshman students?
-What are we doing as an institution to decrease the level of alienation students may experience?
-How many minority students complete their freshman year as compared to whites? Why or why not?

Comments:

7. Financial Aid

This program area includes those activities your institution engages in to assist Minority students with their financial aid needs.

Use this scale to complete your ranking

0	1	2	3	4
not applicable	inadequate	fair	good	excellent

Activity   **Ranking**

a) Lowest income students unmet need fully funded   _____

b) Financial aid workshops offered   _____

c) Students informed of scholarships & other awards
they can apply for   _____

d) Scholarship fundraising campaigns implemented
for minority students   _____

e) Students assisted in finding jobs both on and off
campus   _____

f) Financial aid appeal procedures explained to
students   _____

g) Annual loan debt study conducted and manageable
debt levels established   _____

h) Financial aid information included in recruitment
efforts   _____

i) Exit interviews conducted for dropouts and loan
debt responsibilties explained   _____

j) Other _____   _____

          fill in

k) Where do you feel that financial aid activities should be
placed in terms of priority/resources?

Circle One

0	1 2 3 4 5 6	7 8 9 10 11 12	13 14 15 16 17
unable to answer	high priority	average priority	low priority

l) How effective are your current financial aid efforts?

Circle One

0	1 2 3	4 5 6	7 8
unable to answer	ineffective	adequate	very effective

Discussion Questions:

-How can work study and other student employment opportunities be used to enhance minority student involvement on
campus?
-Do we provide loan debt counseling, budgeting and similiar
services to students and how effective are these services?
-Where can we obtain funds to supplement declining federal
dollars?
-What has been the total aid awarded to minority students
including the average award in relation to white students for
the past five years?

-What is the default rate for minority students in repaying their loans?

-How can we mix our financial aid package to attract eligible minority students?

-Does our institutional financial aid packaging policy ensure that financial aid is distributed equitably?

-Is there an annual loan debt study conducted and if so how does the minority student debt compare with white students?

Comments:

8. Academic Advising

Use this scale to complete your ranking

0	1	2	3	4
not applicable	inadequate	fair	good	excellent

Activity   **Ranking**

a) Students provided with an advisor they can
see regularly   _____

b) Advisors provided appropriate training for
working with minority students   _____

c) Professors informed as to whom the minority
student's advisor is   _____

d) Personalized letters sent to parents of minority
freshmen   _____

e) Student course selection reflects quality advising   _____

Activity   **Ranking**

f) Advisors familiarize students with the basic regulations and procedures such as add/drop deadlines   _____

g) Other   _____   _____
                        fill in

h) Where do you feel that academic advising activities should
be placed in terms of priority/resources?

Circle One

    0   1 2 3 4 5 6   7 8 9 10 11 12   13 14 15 16 17
unable to   high priority   average priority   low priority
answer

i) How effective are your current academic advising efforts?

Circle One

    0   1 2 3   4 5 6   7 8
unable to   ineffective   adequate   very effective
answer

Discussion Questions:

-What type of training is or needs to be offered to ensure that
advisors are sensitive to the needs of minority students?
-What type of monitoring needs to be done to ensure that
minority students are exposed to a wide choice in selecting a
major?
-Should we implement a formal recognition/reward system for
faculty/staff involved in advising?

-Should an advisor's handbook be compiled as a supplemental resource and if so what should be included in it?

-Does minority student scheduling and course selection reflect good advising?

Comments:

9. Counseling/Career Placement

Use this scale to complete your ranking

0	1	2	3	4
not applicable	inadequate	fair	good	excellent

Activity   **Ranking**

a) Counseling office engaged in preventive
outreach efforts   _____

b) Minority students make use of counseling center   _____

c) Peer counselors used in appropriate situations   _____

d) Career Placement office helps students with resume
writing, interviewing skills, etc.   _____

e) Job/Career interest inventories administered by
career placement office   _____

f) Career counseling, workshops and related services
offered   _____

g) Statistics on job placement rates of minority students
kept   _____

Activity	Ranking

h) Other _____   _____
                          fill in

i) Where do you feel that counseling/career placement activities should be placed in terms of priority/resources?

Circle One

0	1 2 3 4 5 6	7 8 9 10 11 12	13 14 15 16 17
unable to answer	high priority	average priority	low priority

j) How effective are your current counseling/career placement efforts?

Circle One

0	1 2 3	4 5 6	7 8
unable to answer	ineffective	adequate	very effective

Discussion Questions:

-To what extent do minority students utilize counseling services? Why?
-How satisfactory is the counseling offered to minority students?
-Are there certain factors counselors should be aware of when counseling minority students?
-What type of additional training should counselors receive in order to better serve minority students?
-Are peer counselors being used and how are they evaluated?

-What insights regarding the retention problem might counsel-
ors have that may be different than faculty and administrators?
-What type of career education is offered by the institution?
What needs to be?

Comments:

10. Learning Resource Center

Use this scale to complete your ranking

0	1	2	3	4
not applicable	inadequate	fair	good	excellent

Activity   **Ranking**

a) Academic difficulties diagnosed early on
_____

b) Linkages established with faculty and various
academic departments
_____

c) Remedial help provided in a non-stigmatized
environment
_____

d) Trained tutors provided
_____

e) Tutoring program monitored and evaluated
annually
_____

f) Adequate space provided for tutorial service and
group study
_____

g) Walk in tutoring available
_____

h) Skill building emphasized
_____

Activity   **Ranking**

i) Self tutoring available via tapes, computers or
other technology   _____

j) Data kept on the number of students served and
type of services rendered.   _____

k) Other _____   _____
                    fill in

l) Where do you feel that the Learning Resource Center
should be placed in terms of priority/resources?

Circle One

    0   1 2 3 4 5 6   7 8 9 10 11 12   13 14 15 16 17
unable to   high priority   average priority   low priority
answer

m) How effective are your Learning Resource Center
Services?

Circle One

    0   1 2 3   4 5 6   7 8
unable to   ineffective   adequate   very effective
answer

Discussion Questions:

-What placement and measurement instruments do we utilize
in assessing minority students? How valid are they?

-What kind of working relationship should the Learning Resource Center or special programs staff have with various academic departments?
-What is the atmosphere like in which remedial programs are
offered? Is there geniune support or is the delivery of such
marred by stigmatization?
-Is academic credit awarded for support service courses?
-Administratively how does the Learning Center and other support programs relate to the academic arm of the campus?
-How is the academic progress of minority students using the
center's service monitored?
-How are students encouraged to use the Learning Resource
Center?

Comments:

11. Faculty Involvement

No improvement can be expected in decreasing the attrition rate without faculty leadership and involvement. Collectively and individually faculty have more power to improve
retention on campuses that any other group.

Use this scale to complete your ranking

0	1	2	3	4
not applicable	inadequate	fair	good	excellent

Activity   **Ranking**

a) Standing committee on minority student recruitment and retention created

_____

b) Out of class activities offered for faculty to interact
with minority students

_____

Activity	Ranking

c) Early warning system in place where faculty informs students' advisors prior to the sixth week of class when student is facing academic difficulty.   _____

d) Faculty involved in minority student activities   _____

e) Institute on Multicultural Curriculum Reform offered in summer to help faculty pluralize class lectures   _____

f) Faculty honored/rewarded for exemplary work with minority students   _____

g) Training provided faculty to enable them to better advise and counsel minority students   _____

h) Other _____   _____
$\qquad$ fill in

i) Where do you feel that faculty involvement should be placed in terms of priority/resources?

Circle One

0	1 2 3 4 5 6	7 8 9 10 11 12	13 14 15 16 17
unable to answer	high priority	average priority	low priority

j) How effective are current faculty involvement activities?

Circle One

0	1 2 3	4 5 6	7 8
unable to answer	ineffective	adequate	very effective

Discussion Questions:

-What approaches should we consider to increase faculty involvement in retention programs? What role should faculty be expected to play?
-In evaluating faculty members how much consideration is given to special duties such as counseling minority students, frequently asked of minority faculty, in addition to their regular duties?
-How can we convince faculty that academic standards won't be lowered in order for retention efforts to work?
-In what ways can we help in pluralizing faculty curriculum and class readings?
-How is research by and about minorities encouraged?
-How does faculty expectations of minority students affect student performance?

Comments:

12. Student Incentives

Use this scale to complete your ranking

0	1	2	3	4
not applicable	inadequate	fair	good	excellent

Activity   **Ranking**

a) Minority student leadership and similar develop-
mental skill workshops offered   _____

b) Student academic "stars" acknowledged/honored   _____

c) Students surveyed regarding their opinions on
minority student services   _____

d) Students involved in retention activities   _____

e) Student study groups/organizations encouraged and
resources (space, telephone, xeroxing) provided   _____

f) Supplemental minority student directory compiled
by class, major, and high school attended to facilitate
social interaction/study groups   _____

g) Other   _____   _____
                        fill in

h) Where do you feel that student incentives should be placed
in terms of priority/resources?

Circle One

0	1 2 3 4 5 6	7 8 9 10 11 12	13 14 15 16 17
unable to	high priority	average priority	low priority
answer			

i) How effective are current student incentive efforts?

Circle One

0	1 2 3	4 5 6	7 8
unable to answer	ineffective	adequate	very effective

Discussion Questions:

-How are students encouraged to join campus organizations and to get involved on campus?
-How much participation is there by minority students in such activities as debate team, campus newspaper, student government, intramural sports and yearbook staff?
-What type of recognition is provided for academic achievement?
-Are minority students aware of the complaint/grievance procedures on campus?
-What attributes within the student contribute toward or hinder his/her retention?

Comments:

13. Social Factors

Use this scale to complete your ranking

0	1	2	3	4
not applicable	inadequate	fair	good	excellent

Activities   **Ranking**

a) Minority cultural activities offered   _____

Activity   **Ranking**

b) University policies evaluated in terms of
institutional racism
                                                          _____

c) Town-gown committee formed to help minority
students adjust to the larger community
                                                          _____

d) Students encouraged to join organizations and
participate in campus activities
                                                          _____

e) Other _____   _____
                              fill in

f) Where do you feel that social factors should be placed in
terms of priority/resources?

Circle One

    0   1 2 3 4 5 6   7 8 9 10 11 12   13 14 15 16 17
unable to   high priority   average priority   low priority
answer

g) How effective are current efforts to address social issues?

Circle One

    0   1 2 3   4 5 6   7 8
unable to   ineffective   adequate   very effective
answer

Discussion Questions:

-How are social problems like racism, alienation, and cultural
conflict dealt with on campus?

-How can we ensure that minority cultural programs become an integral part of the student activities calendar?
-What additional policies should the institution adopt that will require all publications sent to prospective students represent a diverse student population in terms of pictures, etc?
-How is the local community involved in making minority students feel welcome?

Comments:

14. Graduation

This program area includes all those activities your institution engages in to help minority students earn a degree.

Use this scale to complete your ranking.

Not Applicable Inadequate   fair   Good Excellent
       0   1   2   3   4

Graduation Activities   **Ranking**

a) Degree summary made annually informing
students of courses they've taken and need to
graduate
                                                         _____

b) Students encouraged to meet with academic advisors
at least once a semester
                                                         _____

c) Minority student organizations acknowledge/
honor graduating seniors and graduate students
annually
                                                         _____

Graduation Activities   Ranking

d) Minority students/faculty included in graduation
ceremonies   _____

e) Data available on minority student majors, class
rank and monitoring of same   _____

f) Other _____   _____
                        fill in

g) Where do you feel that graduation activities should be
placed in terms of priority/resources?

Circle One

0	1 2 3 4 5 6	7 8 9 10 11 12	13 14 15 16 17
unable to	high priority	average priority	low priority
answer			

h) How effective are overall graduation activities?

Circle One

0	1 2 3	4 5 6	7 8
unable to	ineffective	adequate	very effective
answer			

Discussion Questions:

-What has been our graduation rate, both in terms of actual
numbers and percentages of minority students for the past five
years?
-In what disciplines are graduates majoring in? Why?

-What types of recruitment and retention strategies does the graduate school and various departments use to attract minority students?
-How much emphasis is given to increasing the number of minorities in fields where they are underrepresented?

Comments:

15. Post-Graduation

This program area includes all those activities your institution engages in to assist minority students in obtaining graduate/professional school opportunities.

Use this scale to complete your ranking

Not Applicable	Inadequate	fair	Good	Excellent
0	1	2	3	4

Post Graduation Activities   **Ranking**

a) Fellowship/Teaching Assistantships offered
to minority students
                                                              _____

b) Requirements for graduate school workshops
sponsored by various departments
                                                              _____

c) Information sent to students regarding GRE,
LSAT and similar test dates
                                                              _____

d) Announcements posted in minority student
centers/hangouts
                                                              _____

e) Early identification program created to locate
potential graduate students
                                                              _____

Post Graduation Activities   Ranking

f) Practicum and internship opportunities offered   _____

g) Individual, office or committee identified to recruit
and retain minority graduate students   _____

h) Post-Doctoral opportunities provided for
minorities   _____

i) Other _____   _____
                    fill in

j) Where do you feel that Post-Graduation activities should be
placed in terms of priority/resources?

                    Circle One

    0   1 2 3 4 5 6   7 8 9 10 11 12   13 14 15 16 17
unable to   high priority   average priority   low priority
answer

k) How effective are overall post-graduation activities?

                    Circle One

    0   1 2 3   4 5 6   7 8
unable to   ineffective   adequate   very effective
answer

Discussion Questions:

-How are we doing numbers wise in terms of minority teaching,
research and project assistants?

-How are we getting the word out to prospective minority students about graduate opportunities?

-What can we do to prepare our students to become teaching assistants?

-Is there a role for remedial type programs in graduate school to help additional minority students enter, especially the professions?

-Does existing admissions criteria place an unfair disadvantage on minority students?

-Should special student support services be made available to professional and graduate students?

Comments:

16. Alumni

This program area includes all those activities your institution engages in to encourage minority student alumni involvement.

Use this scale to complete your ranking

Not Applicable Inadequate   fair   Good Excellent
0   1   2   3   4

Alumni Activities   **Ranking**

a) Targeted efforts directed at increasing minority
student involvement
_____

b) Minority alumni advisory body created
_____

c) Both minority and non-minority alumni involved in
minority student retention activities
_____

Alumni Activities   **Ranking**

d) Minority alumni organization created and involved
in retention activities   _____

e) Multicultural wing/bulletin boards, etc. displayed
in alumni house   _____

f) Alumni invited to talk to students from time to
time   _____

g) Minority alumni traditions developed   _____

h) Other _____   _____
                    fill in

i) Where do you feel that alumni activities should be placed in
terms of priority/resources?

Circle One

0	1 2 3 4 5 6	7 8 9 10 11 12	13 14 15 16 17
unable to	high priority	average priority	low priority
answer			

j) How effective are current alumni activities in getting former
minority students involved?

Circle One

0	1 2 3	4 5 6	7 8
unable to	ineffective	adequate	very effective
answer			

Discussion Questions:

-In what ways are alumni currently involved in recruitment and retention efforts? How effective is this involvement?
-Should we encourage the formation of a minority alumni organization?
-How can we ensure that minority alumni involvement will be just as beneficial for the alumni as we hope it is for the institution?
-Should we compile a minority student alumni directory?

Comments:

17. Affirmative Action Efforts

Use this scale to complete your ranking

0	1	2	3	4
not applicable	inadequate	fair	good	excellent

Activity   **Ranking**

a) Entire campus informed that retention is everyone's responsibility via campus-wide retention
committee   _____

b) Research conducted on retention problems and
major factors identified   _____

c) Annual retention report required from each college   _____

d) Retention objectives included in administrator's
contract   _____

e) Affirmative action policy enforced and a pluralistic
staff stated as part of the campus's mission   _____

f) Withdrawal process includes additional intervention
services, gathers data on why students leave and the
exit interview provides the counselor with information
from faculty, residence halls, minority affairs and
applicable student services' offices   _____

g) Minority social activities made an integral part of
the student calendar   _____

h) Ethnic cultural center available for minority
students   _____

i) Data available on attrition/retention rates   _____

j) Other _____   _____
                        fill in

k) Where do you feel that Affirmative Action activities should
be placed in terms of priority/resources?

                       Circle One

      0   1 2 3 4 5 6   7 8 9 10 11 12   13 14 15 16 17
unable to   high priority   average priority   low priority
answer

1) How effective are current Affirmative Action efforts overall?

Circle One

0	1 2 3	4 5 6	7 8
unable to answer	ineffective	adequate	very effective

Discussion Questions:

-Does our institution have a strong Affirmative Action plan in name only?

-Are special academic support services provided for English as a Second Language students?

-Is there support for the institution to sponsor an in house minority student retention conference?

-What are we as an institution doing to encourage attrition and what are we doing to reduce it?

-How is the data that is collected on the number of minority faculty, staff, tenure, etc. used?

-Are there separate or integrated operating policies for minority student programs?

-What is the institution's financial commitment in terms of soft money and hard money in funding minority student services?

-Are minority services programs assured of long term existence, subject to normal evaluations, or are they operating in an unstable environment from year to year?

-What mechanisms are in place to facilitate obtaining advice from minorities about programs that affect them?

-Are minority concerns placed on the presidents, board of trustees and top administrators' agendas periodically?

-Should ethnic minority history courses be mandated?

-Are ethnic studies supported by the institution?

-Are minority suppliers and services used? Minority Bankers? Insurance Companies? Contractors?

-Is there a university committee to develop and implement a nonracist policy?
-Does the affirmative action officer have meaningful access to all department heads and personnel engaged in hiring?
-Is there a designee in every department responsible for departmental Affirmative Action efforts? Does this person act as a liason with the university's Affirmative Action Officer?

Comments:

Evaluation

Retention Program Areas

Now you need to summarize your institution's overall efforts, their effectiveness and prioritize those activities you feel your institution should concentrate on. Using the same effectiveness scale you used to compute previous rankings write in your overall ranking, from lowest to highest on a scale of: (0-8).

Effectiveness Ranking

Circle One

0	1 2 3	4 5 6	7 8
unable to answer	ineffective	adequate	very effective

Priority Ranking

Finally prioritize the activities using a ranking from highest to lowest on a scale of 1-17.

1 2 3 4 5 6	7 8 9 10 11 12	13 14 15 16 17
high priority	average priority	low priority

Activity	Effectiveness Ranking 0-8	Priority Ranking 1-17
A. Pre-Collegiate Activities	_____	_____
B. Recruiting Activities	_____	_____
C. Admission Activities	_____	_____
D. Matriculation Activities	_____	_____
E. Orientation Activities	_____	_____
F. The Freshman Year	_____	_____
G. Financial Aid	_____	_____
H. Academic Advising	_____	_____
I. Counseling/Career Placement	_____	_____
J. Learning Resource Center	_____	_____
K. Faculty Involvement	_____	_____

Activity	Effectiveness Ranking 0-8	Priority Ranking 1-17
L. Student Incentives	_____	_____
M. Social Factors	_____	_____
N. Graduation Activities	_____	_____
O. Post-Graduation Activities	_____	_____
P. Alumni Activities	_____	_____
Q. Affirmative Action Efforts	_____	_____

Conclusion

By now you should have a clearer picture of where your institution stands in terms of effectively servicing the needs of minority students. Ideally you would have also reached consensus on what program components should be given greater priority considerations. Now its time for your institution either through a retention team or some other appropriate body to develop a plan of action to implement those activities you deem appropriate for your campus. This instrument is merely the first step, albeit an extremely important one. Creative leadership and genuine committment will be needed if meaningful results are to occur. One observation should be reemphasized. The very nature of issues presented in this instrument prohibit one person or office from addressing them. It will take the combined efforts of the entire institution for real change to happen.

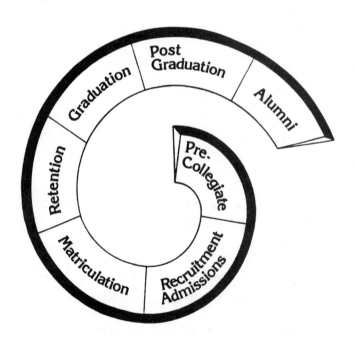

Related Books of Interest

Effective Ways to Recruit and Retain Minority Students
This publication is a must for universities and colleges. It provides a coordinated approach to recruiting and retaining minority students, speaks to factors that create retention problems, features successful programs from around the country and lists dozens of ideas you can implement on your campus immediately. *($29.95)*

How To Sponsor a Minority Cultural Retreat
Looking for ways to break down racial barriers, and ways to get minority and white students to interact, then this book is for you. This handbook shows you step by step how to conduct a retreat and is filled with activities to ensure your retreat's success. *($24.95)*

Guide to Multicultural Resources (1989-90 edition)
The guide is a comprehensive collection of programs, organizations, businesses, services and related information from the Black, Hispanic, Indian, and Asian communities. Anyone wishing to network with the minority community should have this book. Includes names, addresses and phone numbers of hundreds of entries. *($58.00)*

The Handbook of Minority Student Services
Everything students, faculty, and administrators need to establish successful minority programs on campus. A necessary book for student services staff and campus planners. *($49.95)*

To order any of the above books add $3.50 shipping and handling and mail check or money order to:

Praxis Publications Inc.
P.O. Box 9869
Madison, WI 53715

For additional information call 608/244-5633.

NOTES

NOTES